BizTalk 2010 EDI for Health Care

HIPAA Compliant 837 Solutions

Mark Beckner

Apress®

BizTalk 2010 EDI for Health Care: HIPAA Compliant 837 Solutions

An Apress Advanced Book

Copyright © 2013 by Mark Beckner

ISBN-13 (pbk): 978-1-4302-5019-7

ISBN-13 (electronic): 978-1-4302-5021-0

President and Publisher: Paul Manning
Lead Editor: Jeffrey Pepper
Technical Reviewer: Richard Kikuchi
Editorial Board: Steve Anglin, Ewan Buckingham, Gary Cornell, Louise Corrigan, Morgan Ertel, Jonathan Gennick, Jonathan Hassell, Robert Hutchinson, Michelle Lowman, James Markham, Matthew Moodie, Jeff Olson, Jeffrey Pepper, Douglas Pundick, Ben Renow-Clarke, Dominic Shakeshaft, Gwenan Spearing, Matt Wade, Tom Welsh
Coordinating Editor: Anamika Panchoo
Copy Editor: Linda Seifert
Compositor: SPi Global
Indexer: SPi Global
Artist: SPi Global
Cover Designer: Anna Ishchenko

Distributed to the book trade worldwide by Springer Science+Business Media New York, 233 Spring Street, 6th Floor, New York, NY 10013. Phone 1-800-SPRINGER, fax (201) 348-4505, e-mail orders-ny@springer-sbm.com, or visit www.springeronline.com.

For information on translations, please e-mail rights@apress.com, or visit www.apress.com.

Apress and friends of ED books may be purchased in bulk for academic, corporate, or promotional use. eBook versions and licenses are also available for most titles. For more information, reference our Special Bulk Sales–eBook Licensing web page at www.apress.com/bulk-sales.

To my dear wife who home birthed our two boys and is an acupuncturist. Because of your "ideas," we have yet to file a claim for these kids that has been transported through any EDI or claims management processing system, BizTalk or otherwise.

—Mark Beckner

Contents at a Glance

Contents

Foreword

As a health care practitioner, I have never written a line of code, yet I am responsible for orchestrating some of the best health care applications in the industry. Imagine developing an application that pays a doctor for services before the insurance company has even received the bill! That's risky! I know how far I can push the technology envelope and I enjoy salaciously pushing it. I build people advanced technological tools, yet I hunt and peck my own keyboard. Technology to me is a ball you constantly move forward, because if and when it stops, your game is over. The technology covered in this book is the tool to move your technology ball forward.

Since the early eighties, I have been a part of and followed the evolution of both hardware and software. My first computer cost me $10,000, not including a keyboard, monitor, or operating system. I could have bought a car for what I paid for that small, heavy, metal box. I used it to develop my first successful medical billing application. My first experience with electronic data interchange (EDI) came in 1986 and utilized a rudimentary format that failed entire batches of bills because of one missing piece of information. That was bad. On the other hand, I began to receive payments in less than 14 days, and in some cases less than a week. That was good. I speculated that my EDI process bypassed human claim adjusters. I was communicating to the master claims system and my bills were triggering checks. I will never forget one healthcare CIO saying he would have to build in controls to slow down payments because they were being made too fast. Wow. My conclusion—EDI works.

Fast forward 12 years; I built the blueprint for an Iinternet-based EDI system that not only transmitted the universal medical bill HCFA-1500, but would also transmit all supporting medical documents. iHCFA was born. Unfortunately, I realized after reading an article in *Barron's* that I was about 14 years ahead of the industry. One major insurance company after another realized they were saddled with legacy systems unable to utilize the efficiency EDI presented. One more hurdle to overcome.

So, how long does a technological solution last and how quickly does technology improve? It is like a snapshot in time. In my opinion, he who has the better system wins, especially as we become more comfortable with technology and its devices. Steve Jobs made a decision to not allow an iPhone user to change their battery. Was this because he knew the iPhone would last a lifetime, or because he knew his users would become bored and expect something new? Staying ahead of your competition is the key to success.

Once in a while, a technology hits the street that moves application development light years ahead in just a matter of minutes. Why it happens and who funds it is not important. What is important is that someone somewhere saw a need and an opportunity to create something that could standardize an industry. In my world, this technology warp was

Microsoft BizTalk Server, a readily available application with the ability to provide a working nervous system to the complex world of EDI. This is a system which provides the end user the ability to bolt on customized components, rudimentary or sophisticated, and allow the BizTalk infrastructure to take over and guide the data to a proper outcome.

BizTalk becomes an *out of the box* application that enables the user to save years of development time. For me, it became a technically superior product which I could customize in less than six months. The decision to use BizTalk was a simple one. My only deficiency was guidance.

All technology needs is someone capable of navigating through the most treacherous waters. BizTalk, a Microsoft product, provides a plethora of options. At its helm is the man who wrote this book, even though he was 2,000 miles away, Mark Beckner. Mark is a BizTalk expert and he can navigate the BizTalk waters like a beacon in the night. Mark assisted us in implementing BizTalk as the backbone of a new EDI system that would take our healthcare transactions to a new level. Mark utilized the many robust internal features of BizTalk to halve our development time and, in today's highly competitive technology world, this became a differentiator for us.

Mark provided us with stable guidance that allows us to utilize our current system as a blueprint to a new BizTalk-based system. The insight Mark provides is the same insight the reader will find in this book. Mark provides real-time solutions to a complex EDI world, ultimately simplifying the hardest of tasks. Getting to the experts is often half the battle when it comes to development efficiency and Mark has provided his expertise in a transparent, open fashion, enabling anyone to take advantage of BizTalk and its product lines. In my opinion, this book will fast track your success just like BizTalk fast tracked mine.

William J. DeGasperis, DC
President & CEO
Atlantic Imaging Group and iHCFA

About the Author

Mark Beckner is a technical consultant specializing in business strategy and enterprise application integration. He runs his own consulting firm, Inotek Consulting Group, LLC, delivering innovative solutions to large corporations and small businesses. His projects have included engagements with numerous clients throughout the U.S., and range in nature from mobile application development to complete integration solutions. He has authored *BizTalk 2010 Recipes*, *Pro EDI in BizTalk Server 2006 R2*, and *Pro RFID in BizTalk Server 2009*, and has spoken at a number of venues, including Microsoft TechEd. In addition to BizTalk, he works with Microsoft Dynamics CRM, SharePoint, and custom .NET development. Beckner, his wife Sara, and his boys Ciro and Iyer live somewhere in the rugged deserts and/or mountains of the American West. His website is http://www.inotekgroup.com and he can be contacted directly at mbeckner@inotekgroup.com.

About the Technical Reviewer

Richard Kikuchi is an information technology professional with 20 years of experience creating solutions in the healthcare industry. He currently works for a large independent practice association in Southern California as the Director of Information Integration. Richard and his team of database and report developers leverage key Microsoft technologies to create business process efficiencies. He specializes in data warehousing, enterprise reporting, healthcare economics, and electronic data interchange. Richard lives in Orange County, California with his wife, Kelleen, and their two daughters, Brianne and Stacy.

Introduction

There is an immense need within the claims management industry to build highly efficient EDI processing systems that are cost effective and easy to maintain and extend. BizTalk is emerging as the leading technology applied in this space due to its low initial cost and the relative ease with which it can be adopted into infrastructures that are Microsoft based. While the ramp up to be highly proficient with the tool is high, building your own fully HIPAA compliant solution is completely achievable.

My objective in this book is to lay out several common patterns for implementing specific EDI Health Care–based BizTalk solutions, so that you—whether you are an executive, an architect, or a developer—can see all the components required and understand exactly what needs to be developed to build your own specific implementation. My hope is that you can accurately assess the skills that required, the amount of time necessary, and the complexity of the tasks ahead, and that you can enter into the development of your solution with a clear idea of what is required to be successful.

A website dedicated to the application of BizTalk within the health care profession can be found at `http://www.biztalkforhealthcare.com`. You will find an array of topics, both technical and business focused, discussed on this site. It will be available starting in December of 2012.

Contacting the Author

If you have questions about the specifics of what it will take to successfully deliver your own EDI Health Care implementation with BizTalk Server, please contact me at `mbeckner @inotekgroup.com`.

Architectural Patterns   Chapter 1

BizTalk is a development platform that lends itself to a variety of implementation styles. After you've worked with the platform on a number of projects, however, you will find that there are really only a few patterns that meet the critical requirements of a well-developed solution. In this chapter you look at some of the most appropriate architectural patterns for health care implementations, centered on the specific requirements of the Professional Health Care Claim in the 837P 5010 format.

The 837P format is one of the most complex document types in EDI, and requires careful planning to implement correctly. By working through this document format in detail, you can quickly move on to other health care document formats without delay, as they all follow similar patterns. The patterns you will look at include details on:

- Receiving inbound 837P files

- Receiving data via SFTP, FTP, and AS2

- Decrypting inbound data

- Mapping to other 837P versions, proprietary flat file formats, and SQL Server databases

- Returning acknowledgements

- Working with orchestrations

- Sending outbound 837P files

- Mapping from internal flat file formats

- Creating source data from SQL Server

- Encrypting data

- Sending batched and unbatched data

With the architectural patterns outlined in this chapter, you'll then move quickly into actual development of each of the components required within the patterns. Chapter 2 outlines specifics on how to build out a fully functional inbound 837P solution, while Chapter 3 details how to build the outbound process. Detailed information about mapping is given in Chapter 4, and discussions about how to receive and deliver data via various protocols (including AS2) are in Chapter 5.

Receiving Inbound 837P Data

Receiving and processing inbound 837P data can take on a variety of flavors, depending on where the data is coming from, whether it is encrypted, what is being done with the data once BizTalk has it, and what kind of validation and acknowledgements are required. Some of the most common patterns to consuming this data and processing it are outlined in the following sections.

Receiving Data via SFTP

In many health care related businesses, data is exchanged using SFTP. SFTP ensures data is transferred in an encrypted format that allows for HIPAA compliant communication, yet is a simple to implement transfer protocol. Retrieving data via SFTP in BizTalk is very simple, and can be done through several adapters, none of which ship with the core product itself. Details on implementing one of these—the free bLogical adapter available on CodePlex—are given in Chapter 5. The pattern for receiving the 837P data over SFTP is shown in Figure 1-1.

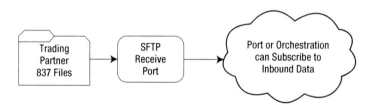

Figure 1-1. Receiving 837P data via an SFTP adapter

Receiving PGP Encrypted Data via FTP

When SFTP is not available, standard FTP is used—however, this protocol is not HIPAA compliant and requires the actual data file to be encrypted. FTP is very easy to implement within BizTalk through the use of the standard FTP adapter, but creating processes to decrypt the data is much more labor intensive and requires coding. The most common approach to handling this is through developing a custom pipeline and pipeline component to do the decryption.

Details on building a decryption pipeline that can be used on an FTP Receive Port are given in Chapter 5. The pattern for receiving the 837P data over standard FTP and decrypting the data through a custom pipeline is shown in Figure 1-2.

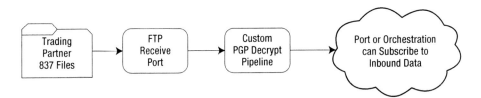

Figure 1-2. Receiving encrypted 837P data via the standard FTP adapter

Receiving Data via AS2

In some cases, data will be exchanged directly between trading partners using AS2. AS2 is a highly secure protocol that allows for various levels of encryption and signing of data. AS2 data is received over HTTP and requires the use of IIS and an HTTP adapter in BizTalk Server. Configuring AS2 is much more involved than is setting up other types of communication protocols, and can lead to fairly lengthy testing cycles with trading partners when used. Chapter 5 details how to implement an inbound AS2 solution. The pattern for receiving the 837P data over AS2 is shown in Figure 1-3.

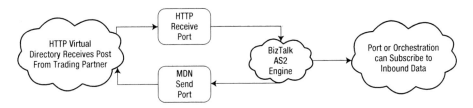

Figure 1-3. Receiving data via AS2

Receiving Data Mapped to Other 837P Formats

Once the 837P data has been received via any protocol, something generally needs to be done with it. In many cases, it is mapped from the original 837P standard into another version of the 837P which can be handled by legacy applications within an IT infrastructure. For example, with the release of version 5010, many companies have to exchange data in the 5010 format, but still have internal applications that deal with the data in the older 4010 version. These applications can directly consume 837P data, but are not 5010 compliant. Therefore, the inbound 837P 5010 format must be downgraded to the 4010 version through BizTalk mapping. Two patterns for receiving the 837P 5010 data and mapping it to the 4010 version are shown in Figure 1-4. One uses a simple Port to Port combination, while the other uses an orchestration to handle the mapping. If you can build a solution without using an orchestration, it will be much easier to support and build. The only reason to use an orchestration is if you have several steps in a workflow that need to be incorporated, or if you have multiple steps in mappings that need to take place.

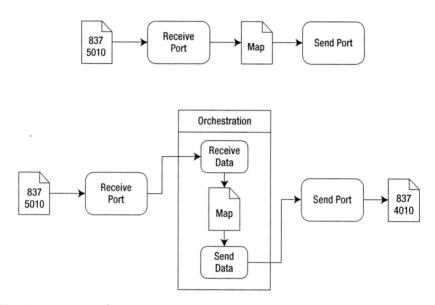

Figure 1-4. Mapping from the 5010 to 4010 version

Receiving Data Mapped to Proprietary Flat Files

Mapping inbound data from the 837P format (regardless of version) to a proprietary flat file format is also extremely common. One example of this is the ECSIF (Electronic Claims Submission Input Format) format, which is used by a variety of claims management systems. Mapping the 837P data to the ECSIF format (or other flat file format) often requires complex manipulations that are best handled with a combination of standard BizTalk mapping, as well as XSLT. Chapter 4 has information on how to handle this mapping, and how to work with XSLT.

Receiving Data Mapped to a SQL Server Database

There are times when the inbound 837P data simply needs to be received and sent directly to a database (or series of databases). There is a huge amount of data available in an 837, and writing this data to tables that reflect this structure in SQL server can require writing to dozens of tables, along with many database lookups. There is really only one appropriate way to handle this kind of complexity within BizTalk, and it consists of a very simple pattern, the use of a stored procedure, and XML.

When the 837P data arrives in BizTalk, it is always converted to an XML structure that represents the EDI document. This XML can be passed directly to a SQL Server stored procedure which can tear apart the XML and insert it into the appropriate tables and databases. The pattern for receiving the 837P data and mapping it directly to a SQL Server database is shown in Figure 1-5.

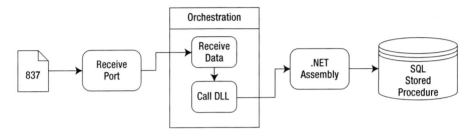

Figure 1-5. Mapping from an 837P to a SQL Server database

Receiving Data that Requires an Acknowledgement

Acknowledgements come in several flavors. The 997/999 (Functional Acknowledgement) is the most common. The technical acknowledgement is also available, but is rarely used by trading partners. The MDN acknowledgement is specific to AS2. All these acknowledgements are easily configured in BizTalk Server, and are automatically generated by the system when they are required. In the case of each of these, a Send Port with an appropriate filter must be set up and certain fields may need to be configured in the Party and Agreement settings within BizTalk. Chapter 5 has details about working with the various acknowledgements. The pattern for sending acknowledgments from BizTalk is shown in Figure 1-6. In this scenario, the trading partner initiates the post of the 837; BizTalk receives it and automatically generates the 997, which is shipped out via a Send Port back to the trading partner.

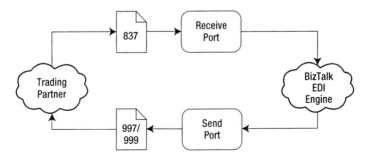

Figure 1-6. Sending Acknowledgements

Receiving Data that Requires an Orchestration

In many cases, there is no need for an orchestration to handle inbound 837P data—the data simply needs to be received, mapped, and dropped in an appropriate format for another subscribing system. In many other cases, it is not enough to simply map and deliver the data without more involved processing—actual workflow steps must take place to handle the data appropriately. In cases where workflow is required, an orchestration must be developed. Examples of implementing orchestrations for common requirements are shown in Chapter 2.

Sending Outbound 837P Files

We've looked at a variety of inbound patterns, now let's look at some outbound patterns. Sending data includes determining where the source data will come from, how this data will be mapped into an 837P format, whether this data will be batched, and how the data will ultimately be delivered. We'll look at a number of outbound patterns that will allow you to develop your outbound 837P solution.

Sending Data Mapped from an Internal Flat File Format

Internal data is often stored by claims management systems, and this data can be readily exported in a variety of formats. In some cases, these systems can export fully compliant 837P documents. In other cases, these systems can export only proprietary representations of the claim data. In either case, this data generally must be mapped to the exact format and standard required by a trading partner. Some trading partners have very lax standards, while others have extremely rigid requirements.

> **Note** There are seven levels of HIPAA EDI Compliance. BizTalk handles level one and two.

In general, all trading partners have their own unique map from whatever internal format you have within your environment to their specific format for the 837P. Even trading partners that have virtually identical 837P format requirements should have a separate map within BizTalk. The pattern for outbound 837P maps based on an internal flat file format is shown in Figure 1-7.

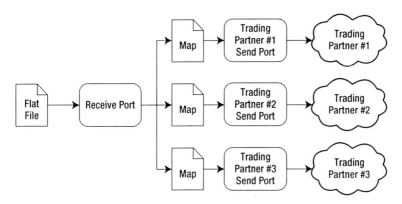

Figure 1-7. Mapping Outbound 837P Data from an Internal Flat File

Sending Data Mapped Directly from SQL Server

When claims data is available in SQL Server databases and tables, there is a fairly straightforward pattern that can be built, which will allow this data to be structured for ease of mapping to 837P by a SQL stored procedure. This data can be retrieved from the stored procedure by BizTalk, mapped to the 837P format, and delivered.

The maps can often be extremely simple when using this pattern, as all the data can be preprocessed and delivered to BizTalk by the stored procedure in the format required by the targeted trading partner. Instead of having logic in functoids and within the map, this logic can reside in SQL, and the maps can remain as simple as possible. Examples of building a stored procedure and mapping the contents to an outbound 837P are shown in Chapter 3. The pattern for handling this type of scenario is shown in Figure 1-8.

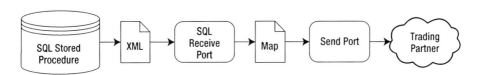

Figure 1-8. Mapping Outbound 837P Data from SQL Server

Sending Unencrypted Data via SFTP

SFTP is a secure file transfer protocol, and files sent over SFTP can be unencrypted and still be HIPAA compliant. Sending files via SFTP requires a third-party adapter, as BizTalk does not ship with an SFTP adapter. Chapter 5 gives details on how to work with one of the available SFTP adapters. The pattern for sending unencrypted 837P data via SFTP is shown in Figure 1-9.

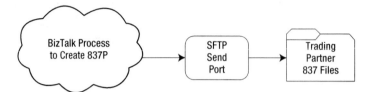

Figure 1-9. Sending Data via SFTP

Sending Encrypted Data via FTP

Data sent over the standard FTP protocol—which is very common within the health care world—must be encrypted for it to be HIPAA compliant. Encrypting data requires the use of a custom pipeline and custom pipeline component, which can be added directly to an FTP Send Port using the FTP adapter that ships with BizTalk. You can look at the discussions in Chapter 5 for more information on how to build out custom pipelines and pipeline components for encryption and decryption. The pattern for sending encrypted data via FTP is shown in Figure 1-10.

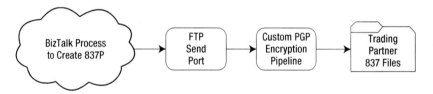

Figure 1-10. Sending encrypted data via standard FTP

Sending Batched Data

There are a number of options around batching data, the two most common examples for 837P being multiple claim records per ST/SE and single claim records per ST/SE. Trading partners dictate their requirements around batching, including maximum number of claims in a file, maximum number of claims in a batch, maximum number of batches in a file, and so on. Dealing with these can often require major shifts in the way you build the same processes for different partners. For example, sending single claims per ST/SE requires a different set of maps and other components than sending multiple claims per ST/SE. A detailed analysis and examples for implementing batching have been outlined in Chapter 3.

Conclusion

There are a wide variety of patterns to dealing with 837P data. This chapter has outlined some of the most common and has pointed to where in this book you'll be able to find more details. In addition to the specifics around how to receive and send data via various protocols, how to encrypt and decrypt files, how to batch, and how to include orchestrations, you'll also need to know how to configure trading partners as BizTalk parties, and how to set up the core EDI functionality within BizTalk. In the next two chapters you will look at specific implementations of receiving and sending 837P data, both of which touch on many components of the various architectures just outlined.

Solution: Receiving 837P Data

In this chapter you walk through a complete end-to-end solution on how to build out BizTalk to receive 837P documents from an external trading partner and send an acknowledgement back. The data is received via an SFTP adapter, archived using a .NET assembly, processed by an orchestration, and written to a flat file in the ECSIF format. You are introduced to many of the key concepts required in virtually any environment that you may find yourself having to develop within. The overview of this specific solution is shown in Figure 2-1.

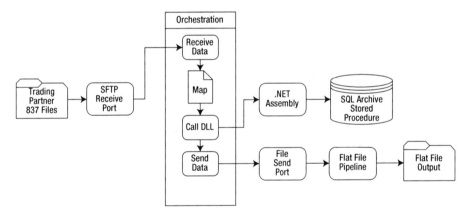

Figure 2-1. Inbound 837P solution overview

Visual Studio Solution

It is critical that your project structure and namespaces are correct from the start. If these are not exactly what you need for the proper architecture and organization of your solution, you'll be spending a great deal of time later in the process rewriting and retesting. For this solution, the namespace is in a structure that you should be able to use directly within your own solutions, substituting the wording, but not the structure. You will also be creating a Visual Studio project structure that will be generic enough to fit within any model you may find yourself confronted with. In the case of the solution being built out, the following Visual Studio projects and namespaces will be used:

- *Solution Name:* Company.BizTalk. This is a generic solution that can hold inbound and outbound projects (see Chapter 3). There are several projects that are common to many projects, so having everything in one solution can be very helpful.

- *Schemas:* There are two schemas used in this solution - the 837P 5010 schema that ships with BizTalk, and the proprietary ECSIF schema.
  ° The 837P schema is contained in its own project. The project name for this is Company.BizTalk.Schemas.X837P.
  ° The ECSIF schema is contained in its own project. The project name for this is Company.BizTalk.Schemas.ECSIF.

Note When setting a namespace, never use a numeric value alone without at least one leading text character (such as the 837 in Company.BizTalk. Schemas.837), as it results in a variety of potential naming conflicts, unexpected errors, and challenges in testing. If you want to refer to an EDI document type directly in your namespace, use a pattern such as a leading "X", such as X837P.

- *Maps:* The map project contains all maps and XSLT required by the solution, and has a namespace of Company.BizTalk.Maps.X837.Inbound.

- *Helper Library:* There is one external .NET assembly project with the namespace of Company.BizTalk.Helper.

- *Orchestration:* There is one orchestration used, which is in its own project called Company.BizTalk.Orchestrations.X837.Inbound.

- *Pipeline:* There is one custom Send pipeline project, which is called Company. BizTalk.Pipelines.X837.Outbound.

The Schema Projects

There are two schemas required for this project. The first is the 837P 5010 schema that ships with BizTalk. BizTalk has thousands of EDI schemas that come with it, crossing all the document types and versions available. There are a number of 837P schemas, so it can be tricky to choose the right one when you are first getting started. Take the following steps to create a project that has the correct 837P BizTalk schema for your implementation:

1. Create a new project in Visual Studio called Company.BizTalk.Schemas. X837P.

2. Find the HIPAA folder in the BizTalk EDI schema collection. There are two versions available: 4010 and 5010. You use the 5010 for this chapter. Click on the 837P folder and notice there is a "single" and a "multiple" available for selection. The schema you need to use depends on your batching requirements (if you have any).

3. If you are receiving a batched 837P, for example, which needs to be split into individual documents, you would use the "multiple" version. Generally, the best approach is to start with the "single" version and if you find that batching is not working the way you would expect it to, experiment with the "multiple" version. Once you have found the correct XSD, add it to your Visual Studio schema project.

Note To access the EDI schemas with BizTalk, browse to the Microsoft BizTalk Server 2010 root folder and go to XSD_Schema\EDI. In this directory you will find a file called MicrosoftEdiXSDTemplates.exe. Running this file extracts all available schemas.

---

4. The second schema project contains the proprietary ECSIF file schema structure. ECSIF files were very common on older claims management systems, and are a flat file structure, and are referred to here and in several mapping discussions in this book. However, don't let this name mislead you—any flat file that you may need to create a schema for will follow the exact same pattern as what is required for the ECSIF—just substitute your flat file name where appropriate. An example of the ECSIF schema structure is shown in Figure 2-2.

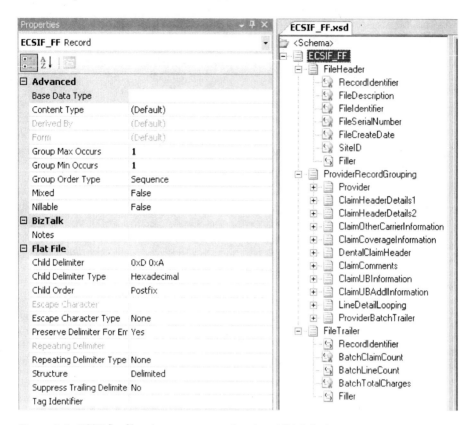

Figure 2-2. ECSIF flat file schema structure showing child delimiter

The steps required for the creation of the ECSIF project are as follows:

1. Create a new project in Visual Studio called Company.BizTalk.Schemas. ECSIF.

2. Add a schema to your project that matches the flat file structure you are after. Any flat file schema that you may need to create can be created using BizTalk's Flat File Schema Wizard, available when you add a new item to your Visual Studio project and select Schema Files. The wizard is pretty involved, and allows for virtually any structure, simple or complex; however, figuring out how to configure things to produce the schema you are after can be a challenge. There are a number of great resources available on the Internet to help you work with this wizard. Search for BizTalk Flat File Schema Wizard to find these links.

The schema projects (especially the X837P) are the foundation of many of the other projects you will be creating, as these other projects reference them. If the schemas change during the course of development, all the other projects will be impacted. Do everything you can to get the schemas namespaced correctly and structured correctly (you don't have to worry about the structure of the 837P schema, but you do have to deal with any schemas you are creating from scratch) at the start of your development.

The Map Project

The map project allows for the mapping of the inbound 837P data into the ECSIF format. Because the ECSIF supports multiple claims, and the 837P contains multiple claims, there is no need for any splitting of the data before it arrives. The 837P data can simply be mapped into the target ECSIF format using whatever mapping techniques are required. That being said, mapping 837P data can be one of the most challenging mapping exercises that you will face—this is not because of BizTalk, but rather because of the enormity in size and structure of data that represents the claims within the 837P.

Chapter 4 in this book is dedicated to the activity of mapping, and looks at the specifics of what is required for the ECSIF (or other flat file) structure. Please refer to that chapter to build out the correct map.

The map project structure should be as follows:

- Create a new project in Visual Studio called Company.BizTalk.Maps.X837. Inbound.

- Add a reference to the two schema project you have created, as you will map from 837P to ECSIF.

The .NET Assembly Project and Related SQL Objects

The .NET helper library is used by the orchestration to archive the inbound XML version of the EDI file to a database in its native XML format. This is an invaluable way of accessing and reporting on data through SQL Business Intelligence (BI) platforms such as SSRS without having to push the 837P data to a traditional database model. The .NET class has a single method and looks similar to the code shown in Listing 2-1. You can pass as many or as few parameters as you would like, depending on the needs of your reporting. The items built within this section are

- A method in a .NET Library that calls a stored procedure

- A stored procedure that inserts data into a table for archiving

> **Note** Always mark your .NET classes as Serializable, so that they can be called from anywhere within BizTalk. To do this, type [Serializable] directly above the class declaration in your helper library.

Listing 2-1. Method Called from Orchestration to Archive Data to SQL

```
public void ArchiveInboundData(string
strSourceFileName, string
strTradingPartner, XmlDocument xmlSource, string
strConnectionString)
{
 SqlConnection sqlConnection = new
SqlConnection(strConnectionString);
 SqlCommand sqlCommand = sqlConnection.CreateCommand();
 sqlCommand.CommandText = "spInsertInboundData";
 sqlCommand.CommandType = CommandType.StoredProcedure;
 sqlConnection.Open();

 SqlParameter sqlParameter = new SqlParameter();

 sqlParameter.ParameterName = "@vchSourceFileName";
 sqlParameter.SqlDbType = SqlDbType.VarChar;
 sqlParameter.Direction = ParameterDirection.Input;
 sqlParameter.Value = strSourceFileName;
 sqlCommand.Parameters.Add(sqlParameter);

 sqlParameter = new SqlParameter();
 sqlParameter.ParameterName = "@vchTradingPartner";
 sqlParameter.SqlDbType = SqlDbType.VarChar;
 sqlParameter.Direction = ParameterDirection.Input;
 sqlParameter.Value = strTradingPartner;
 sqlCommand.Parameters.Add(sqlParameter);

 sqlParameter = new SqlParameter();
 sqlParameter.ParameterName = "@xmlSourceData";
 sqlParameter.SqlDbType = SqlDbType.Xml;
 sqlParameter.Direction = ParameterDirection.Input;
 sqlParameter.Value = new XmlNodeReader(xmlSource);
 sqlCommand.Parameters.Add(sqlParameter);

 sqlCommand.ExecuteNonQuery();
 sqlConnection.Close();
}
```

The stored procedure called from this method is shown in Listing 2-2. It simply takes the data passed to it and inserts it into a table. After the data is in the table, it can be queried using standard T-SQL and XQuery. An example of querying the 837P XML data for the Clearing House Trace Number (a common unique identifier for submitted claims) is shown in Listing 2-3.

Listing 2-2. Stored Procedure to Archive 837P XML Data

```
CREATE PROCEDURE [spInsertInboundData]
 @vchSourceFileName As varchar(500)
 ,@vchTradingPartner As varchar(50)
 ,@xmlSourceData As xml
AS
BEGIN

 SET NOCOUNT ON;
 INSERT tblInboundData
 (
 vchSourceFileName
 ,vchTradingPartner
 ,xmlSourceData
 ,dtmCreateDate
 )
 VALUES
 (
 @vchSourceFileName
 ,@vchTradingPartner
 ,@xmlSourceData
 ,getdate()
 )
END
```

Listing 2-3. Using XQuery to Query Archived 837P XML

```
-- THE FOLLOWING WILL REMOVE NAMESPACE FOR EASE OF
QUERYING
SELECT CAST(REPLACE(CAST(@xmlSourceData As
varchar(max)),'ns0:','')
 As xml) As SourceData
INTO #XML

-- THE FOLLOWING USES XQUERY TO RETRIEVE SPECIFIC VALUE
SELECT DCN.value('REF02__ClearinghouseTraceNumber[1]',
'varchar(255)') As DCN
FROM #XML
CROSS APPLY SourceData.nodes('//REF_TS837Q1_2300_
SubLoop') As header(head)
CROSS APPLY head.nodes('REF_
ClaimIdentificationNumberForClearingHouses
 AndOtherTransmissionIntermediaries_TS837Q1_2300') as
DCN(DCN)
WHERE DCN.value('REF02__ClearinghouseTraceNumber[1]','var
char(255)') IS NOT
NULL
```

After you have the .NET helper library built, you can reference the DLL in the orchestration project and call it to archive the inbound XML data. The next section shows how to call this referenced DLL from within an orchestration.

The Orchestration Project

In this solution, the orchestration receives the 837P directly, maps it, archives it to the database, and sends it out in the final ECSIF format to a file directory. If archiving to the database was not a requirement, all this could be accomplished without the use of an orchestration—the mapping could occur directly on either the Receive Port or Send Port. However, for this solution, the orchestration is used, and an example of it is shown in Figure 2-3. For this orchestration to work, you must add a reference to the .NET Helper DLL, the two schema projects, and the map project, all created earlier in this chapter.

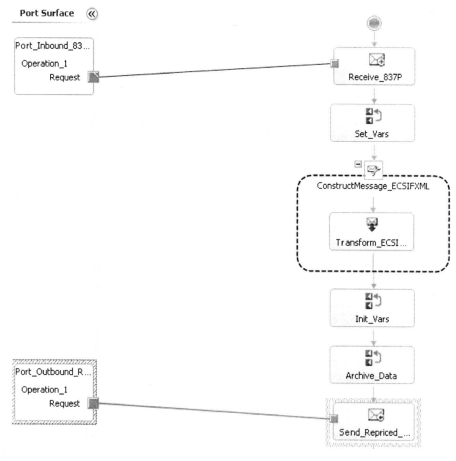

Figure 2-3. The orchestration

Details behind each of the shapes in this orchestration must be given, as several of them are Expression Shapes and have important code behind them. There is no restriction as to how you populate your Expression Shapes, and no requirements as to naming standards. In the case of this orchestration, all the Expression Shapes could be merged into one—but keeping them separate allows you to see how you can add additional message types to this orchestration and reuse common code.

The Receive_837P Shape

This is a simple receive shape that must be set to an orchestration message type of the 837P schema (you need to add a reference to this schema project from your orchestration project). Call this message InboundData. The Activate property on this shape must be set to True.

The Set_Vars Shape

This shape sets variables that are specific to the document just received, and which are immediately available to the orchestration (as opposed to the Init_Vars shape which gets its data from a configuration file). The code behind this shape sets several of the fields that are passed as parameters to archive the data. The code, with notes, is shown in Listing 2-4.

Listing 2-4. Set_Vars Expression Shape Code

```
// Get the Trading Partner ID (from the party settings)
directly off the
// inbound file
strTradingPartnerID = msg837P(EDI.ISA06);

// Several options for getting the file name
strFileIdentifier = System.IO.Path.
GetFileName(msg837P(FILE.ReceivedFileName));
strReceivedFileName = msg837P(FILE.ReceivedFileName);

// getting the original inbound message as XML into a
parameter of type XML
// which can be passed into the helper class and written
to the database as XML
xmlOriginalEDI = new System.Xml.XmlDocument();
xmlOriginalEDI = (System.Xml.XmlDocument)msg837P;
```

The Init_Vars Shape

This shape is used to read from the BizTalk configuration file. There are often variables that are best kept configurable—in this case, the configurable field is the database connection string used to connect to the SQL Server database where the data will be archived. Adding a key/value pair to your configuration file allows for rapid access and alteration of this key. Using the BizTalk configuration file can be done as follows:

- Browse to the root BizTalk Server folder.

- Open BTSNTSvc.exe.config in a plain text editor.

- You can add new configurable fields to the <appSettings> node of this document. An example of storing a connection string would be:

  <add key=" Company.BizTalk.Archiving.ConnectionString" value="Data Source=BTSSQLSERVER;Initial Catalog=Archiving;Integrated Security=SSPI;" />.

- Save the modified config file and restart the BizTalk Host Instance. The field can now be referenced from an Expression Shape using the code shown in Listing 2-5.

Listing 2-5. Init_Vars Expression Shape Code

```
strConnectionString = System.Configuration.
ConfigurationSettings.AppSettings ["Company. BizTalk.
Archiving.ConnectionString"];
```

The Archive_Data Shape

This shape calls the code in the .NET library to do the actual archiving, passing in several fields as parameters. These parameters include the source file name, the trading partner, and the data to be archived. The data being archived in this case is the XML version of the 837P data, readily available to the orchestration in the inbound message. The code for archiving is shown in Listing 2-6. Notice that the inbound message (which is the orchestration message of type Company.BizTalk. Schemas.X837P received on the Receive shape) can be converted to XML and sent straight in as a parameter.

Listing 2-6. Archive_Data Expression Shape Code

```
// the parameter shown here have all been set in previous
shapes
objHelper.ArchiveInboundData(strReceivedFileName,
strTradingPartnerID, (System.Xml.XmlDocument) InboundData,
strConnectionString);
```

Figure 2-4 is a variation of the orchestration that shows receiving an additional document type of the 837I on a Listen shape and sharing the calls to the Init_Data and Archive_Data Expression Shapes. The Listen shape allows for the orchestration to accept more than one type of inbound document. In this case, the Listen shape is receiving 837P data on the left branch and in parallel is listening for 837I data on the right branch. Data coming in on the listener instantiates an instance of the orchestration and executes the code.

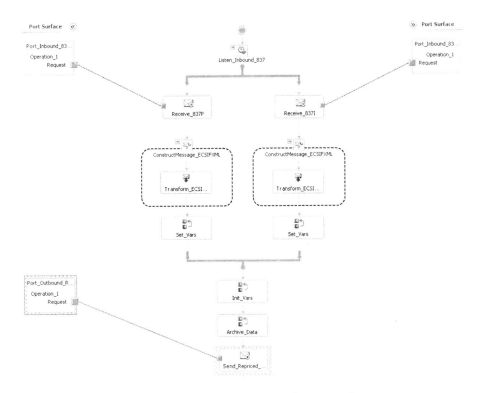

Figure 2-4. A variation on the orchestration with shared common shapes

The Pipeline Project

The final project required is a simple custom flat file pipeline using the Flat File Disassembler component that ships with BizTalk. The use of this pipeline on a Send Port allows the outbound ECSIF document to be output in flat file format. The steps to create this pipeline are as follows, and the pipeline is shown in Figure 2-5.

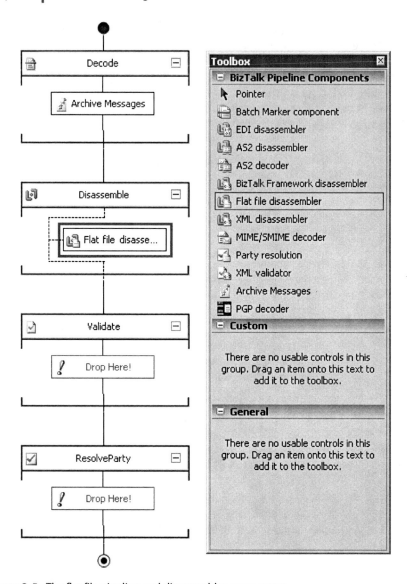

Figure 2-5. The flat file pipeline and disassembler component

1. Create a new project called Company.BizTalk.Pipelines.X837.Outbound.

2. Add a new Send Pipeline to this project.

3. In the pipeline GUI interface, drop a Flat File Disassembler component on the Disassemble stage.

4. In the properties of the disassembler component, set the Document Schema property to the Company.BizTalk.Schemas.ECSIF schema created earlier in this project (you may have to deploy the schema DLL to have access to this).

Setting Up the BizTalk Components

With all the Visual Studio projects completed, you now have a number of BizTalk components to deploy and configure. These components include EDI Party settings, ports, and the orchestration. The first step is to deploy the DLLs that are created when you compile your Visual Studio projects. This can be done in a variety of ways, but the one which allows you the most control (and is the quickest) is as follows. This can be used for adding new DLLs and for updating existing DLLs. After you deploy, always restart the BizTalk Host Instance.

- Open BizTalk Administration Console and browse to the Application where your code will be deployed. If one doesn't exist, create one called Company. BizTalk.

- Right-click the Application and select Add, and then BizTalk Assemblies.

- In the window that opens, click the Add button and add all the assemblies for this solution: two schema DLLs, one map DLL, one orchestration DLL, and the .NET helper DLL.

- Click the Overwrite All checkbox.

- Click on each DLL and make sure the first and third checkbox in the Option window is selected for each one. You must do this for every DLL that you are adding. Figure 2-6 shows the checkboxes being set (the first and third also need to be checked for the .NET assembly, although it has several additional boxes).

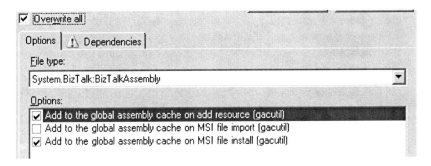

Figure 2-6. The options to select when deploying assemblies

> ▓ **Note** It can be helpful to have all your Visual Studio projects write their compiled DLLs to the same directory, as you deploy them to BizTalk frequently for testing. This can be done by going into the project properties for each project and setting the Output Path of the build to a common directory, such as a custom folder called Binaries.

Party Settings and Agreements

The steps to configure the BizTalk Party settings that contain all the information about how the data will be validated and what the 837P envelope settings should be are as follows:

- Create a new BizTalk Party that represents your home organization. For now, this is called Company. All you need to set is the name.

- Create a new BizTalk Party for your trading partner—this is named Trading Partner for this solution. You need to set up one Party for every trading partner you will be doing business with. Only the name needs to be set.

- Create one Agreement that represents the exchange of information between your trading partner and your company. Right-click the Company Party and create a new Agreement. Set the Protocol type to X12, the First Party is automatically be set to Company, and the second Party is set to your Trading Partner Party. The moment this is done, two additional tabs appear within the Agreement. One tab is for inbound data from the trading partner to your company, while the other is for outbound data from your company to the trading partner.

- On the tab representing inbound data from the trading partner to your company, click the Identifiers, Envelopes, and Character set tabs and enter the appropriate information as required by the 837P envelope. You can easily access this either in a sample instance coming from the trading partner (just open in Notepad and match the values) or by referencing the trading partner implementation guide (if you have one).

- On the Validation tab, set the Transaction Type property to 837_P - Health Care Claim: Professional.

- On the Envelopes tab, set the following values:
  ° Transaction Type should be 837_P - Health Care Claim: Professional.
  ° Version/Release should be 00501 (or 00401 if you are using the 4010 version)

- ° Target namespace should be `http://schemas.microsoft.com/BizTalk/EDI/X12/2006`
- ° GS1 should be HC-Health Care Claim (837)
- ° GS2, GS3, GS4, and GS5 should be set based on what your trading partner requires (again, see the trading partner implementation guide or a sample 837P instance from them)
- ° GS7 should be X-Accredited Standards Committee X12
- ° GS8 should be 005010X222.

Note The GS8 property value can be tricky to get right. If you are batching, or you have a trading partner that requires a certain value here, you may find that you have to create a custom pipeline to override this value right before it is sent to the trading partner.

The Receive Port

The inbound data is received on an SFTP receive port. The details for configuring this port (with and without decrypted data) are given in Chapter 5. What is important to know here is that the port must not only be created, but must be bound to the orchestration. The steps for creating and binding this port are as follows:

1. Create a Receive Port called Company.BizTalk.Receive.X837P.TradingPartner. This allows for a pattern that supports multiple trading partners, if needed.

2. Add a Receive Location to this port and call it the same thing as the Receive Port. Make it type SFTP and configure the appropriate settings for the SFTP connection. Because unencrypted 837P data will be received here, set the Receive pipeline to EdiReceive.

The File Send Port

The Send Port is used to send the final ECSIF flat file that was mapped in the orchestration. The Send Port should be of type File, and should have the Send Pipeline property set to the Company.BizTalk.Pipelines.X837.Outbound pipeline created earlier. This Send Port should be called Company.BizTalk.Send.ECSIF.

Orchestration Binding

The orchestration is set to pick up a file of type 837P, map it to ECSIF, archive it, and then send out the ECSIF document. Once it has been deployed, it needs to be bound to the appropriate Receive and Send Ports. Take the following steps to bind the orchestration to the ports that were just created:

1. In the BizTalk Administration Console, in the Application where you are working, click the Orchestrations folder and open the Company.BizTalk. Orchestrations.X837.Inbound orchestration you have built and deployed.

2. Click the Bindings tab and set the Host property to the BizTalk Server Application host that is available.

3. Set the Receive Port property to the Receive Port you created called Company.BizTalk.Receive.X837P.Receive.

4. Set the Send Port property to the Send Port you created called Company. BizTalk.Send.ECSIF.

5. Click OK to save these settings.

Enabling and Running the Solution

At this point, all the components have been deployed and set up. All you need to do is enable your Receive Location for the inbound SFTP, start your Send Port for the outbound ECSIF flat file, and enable your orchestration. All this can be done through the BizTalk Administration Console. Be sure and restart the BizTalk Host Instance so that all the most current settings and assemblies are loaded into memory.

Conclusion

You have just worked through a full implementation for receiving 837P data and mapping it to an internal proprietary flat file format (ECSIF). Receiving data and getting it into your system is sometimes all there is to an implementation. Other times, sending data back out to trading partners is required. The next chapter focuses on a specific implementation of sending 837P data to a trading partner, and introduces a number of topics not covered in this chapter.

Solution: Sending 837P Data

Chapter 3

In the previous chapter you looked at inbound 837P data—this chapter you will look at outbound 837P data. It introduces how to pull data from a source SQL Server database, map that data to an outbound 837P document, and batch the results into one file with multiple claims per ST/SE. There is important information presented about how best to interact with SQL from BizTalk, how to structure the source data you'll be mapping from, and how to batch the data using configurations available in the BizTalk Party Agreement. The architectural overview of this solution is shown in Figure 3-1.

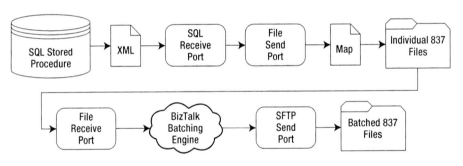

Figure 3-1. Outbound 837P solution overview

It is important to note the pattern for batching. First, the data is retrieved by a SQL Adapter, and then sent out to a file directory by a Send Port in the 837P format. Over the course of a day, the SQL Adapter runs every hour, and during that hour all claims that may have stacked up are retrieved and written out to a single 837P file. BizTalk batching is set to trigger once a day, which means there could be up to 24 individual 837P files written to the file directory and picked up by the batching Receive Port. When the BizTalk batch triggers, the 24 individual 837P files are combined into a single 837P file with 24 ST/SE segments, each containing one or more records.

> ▨ **Note** There are a variety of batching patterns that may be required and that can be built and configured in BizTalk with varying degrees of difficulty. This solution demonstrates how to create one batched 837P file with multiple ST/SE segments containing one or more claim records.

Visual Studio Solution

As discussed in the previous chapter, namespaces and project structure are essential to a successful project, so always take time in the beginning to think through all the components required and how best to name and organize them. Trying to change namespaces and project organization later in the development cycle is especially frustrating with BizTalk, given the number of components and complexity of testing. For this solution, the following Visual Studio projects and namespaces are used:

- *Solution Name:* Company.BizTalk. You can use the same solution you used for the project in Chapter 2.

- *Schemas:* There are two schemas that used in this solution, as follows:
  ° The 837P Schema, which is contained in its own project. This project was created in Chapter 2, and is called Company.BizTalk.Schemas.X837P.
  ° The schema that matches the source SQL data result set. This project's name is Company.BizTalk.Schemas.SQLData.

- *Maps:* The map project contains all maps and XSLT required by the solution, and has a namespace of Company.BizTalk.Maps.X837.Outbound.

The Schema Projects

There are two schemas required for this project. The first is the 837P 5010 schema that ships with BizTalk, and that was discussed in Chapter 2. The second schema project contains the schema that matches how data will be pulled from SQL Server. This is a structure that you have complete control over, and therefore should match as closely is possible the structure of the outbound 837P schema.

The closer you can match the structure and hierarchy, the less complicated the mapping is. You are not required to make it look the same, but the less effort you spend on creating a solid source structure that patterns your claim data properly, the more effort you will spend in mapping and creating code to get this claim data into the target EDI document.

To define the schema for the source data coming from SQL, you want to work through the creation of a result set. The approach that allows for the most extensive flexibility around retrieving data, performing some level of data validation or cleansing, and formatting it in a "BizTalk friendly" way is through the use of a stored procedure.

If you have not used XML within SQL Server before, you are going to want to learn how, as it is essential to building solid, easy to maintain solutions within BizTalk. The stored procedure that you use for this current solution is structured in the following way:

- Retrieve data directly from databases and structure it in a mapping ready format.

- Use FOR XML PATH to give a specific structure to the data and return the result set in XML.

- Use WITH XMLNAMESPACES to ensure it has a unique namespace and contains namespace prefixes that are immediately useable by a BizTalk Schema.

By using a stored procedure, you have endless options on structuring and returning data. You can use a single stored procedure to return data for all outbound trading partners, limit which trading partner is pulled at any given time through a parameter (or set of parameters), and apply specific logic to individual fields to prepare them for being delivered in the outbound 837P. An example of a stored procedure that can pull results in the XML format required by BizTalk is shown in Listing 3-1.

The actual structure of the data shown here is only to demonstrate how to write the procedure—you will want a much more robust and complex structure to the source XML, which matches the requirements of your specific implementation in order to successfully create the outbound 837P document.

Listing 3-1. An Example of a Stored Procedure to Return XML

```
CREATE PROCEDURE [dbo].[RetrieveClaimData]
-- namespace will be used within Schema and should match
your pattern
WITH XMLNAMESPACES('http://Company.BizTalk.SQLSource'
as "ns0")
-- top level is set to NULL
SELECT NULL
, (SELECT c.Type As [ns0:ClaimType].
,c.Number As [ns0:ClaimNumber]
,c.ServiceDate As [ns0:ServiceDate]
, (SELECT p.ProviderFirstName As [ns0:FName]
,p.ProviderLastName As [ns0:LName]
,p.ProviderID As [ns0:BDate]
FROM Providers p
```

```
WHERE p.ID = c.ProviderID
FOR XML PATH('ns0:Provider'), TYPE)
FROM SourceClaimInformation c
FOR XML PATH('ns0:Claim'), TYPE)
FOR XML PATH('ns0:SQLSourceClaims'), TYPE
END
```

Running this stored procedure from SQL Enterprise Manager produces an XML document that can be used to generate your BizTalk schema, or you can create both manually. The creation of this stored procedure and the structuring of the outbound data should be the most difficult task that you have—not in development, but in business analysis and testing. If you get the structure right here, you will save a tremendous amount of time in the actual mapping and testing of data within BizTalk.

After you have the source XML and schema structure worked out, you'll need to add it to a Visual Studio project. For this solution, it will be called Company.BizTalk. Schemas.SQLData.

The Map Project

You have a single map for the outbound process, which maps the source data returned by SQL Server to the target 837P structure. Details for mapping the 837P are given in Chapter 4.

Note If you deliver multiple document types—such as 837 Professional, Institutional, and Dental—to multiple trading partners, you might want to explore the idea of mapping the source data from SQL Server to a canonical structure, and the canonical structure to the target 837P. A canonical structure is a "common" intermediary structure that is a combination of the structure of the source and the target schemas, and allows for a more generic modeling of data. In some cases, you can reduce overall long-term development through the use of a canonical schema, though short term it will increase development efforts and testing requirements.

The map project structure should be as follows:

- Create a new project in Visual Studio called Company.BizTalk.Maps.X837. Outbound.

- Add a reference to the two schema project you have created, as you will be mapping from the source SQL data to the 837P schema.

Setting Up the BizTalk Components

There are fewer Visual Studio components in this outbound solution, but there are more that must be configured within BizTalk, especially around the batch settings in the Party Agreement. You need to set up a SQL Receive Port to pull the data from the stored procedure, a File Send Port to write this data out as an individual 837P, another Receive Port to pick it back up for batching, and a second Send Port to send the batched data when the BizTalk batch fires.

Before configuring these components, you will want to deploy your Visual Studio assemblies to the BizTalk Application. Steps for doing this are outlined in Chapter 2.

SQL Receive Port

The stored procedure that you created earlier in this chapter returns XML—now you need to set up the Receive Port to pull this data into BizTalk. In general, interacting with SQL Server from BizTalk is best done through custom .NET components—the use of the SQL Adapters generally cause bloated, difficult to maintain solutions. However, in the case of pulling XML data from a stored procedure, you can use the SQL Adapter as a simple pass-through mechanism that can be scheduled to run on a periodic basis. You won't have to create any of the additional schemas that generally come with using the SQL adapter to retrieve data. The steps for setting up the SQL Receive Port and Receive Location are as follows (see Figure 3-2):

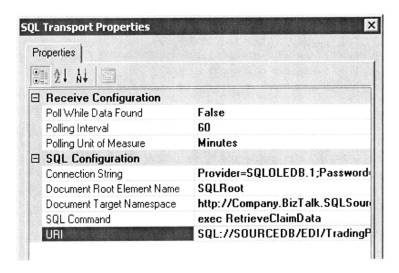

Figure 3-2. The configured SQL receive settings

1. Create a Receive Port called Company.BizTalk.Receive.SourceSQLXML.

2. Add a Receive Location to this port and call it the same thing as the Receive Port. Make it of type SQL. Click Configure next to the SQL Type, and set the following properties:

   - Poll While Data Found should be False.

   - Polling Interval and Polling Unit of Measure should be values that represent how often you want to pull the data from SQL.

   - Connection String is the connection to the database where your stored procedure sits.

   - Document Root Element Name is a wrapped element that is used *only* to allow for the adapter to pull the results. It needs to be the root node of your schema that you have created for the stored procedure results.

> **Note** The schema in Company.BizTalk.Schemas.SQLData should exactly match the structure of the XML returned by the stored procedure, except in that the root node must match what you set in the Document Root Element Name property. So, if the root node of your XML result set from the stored procedure is SQLSourceClaims, and the Document Root Element Name property is SQLRoot, then your schema will need to be SQLRoot/SQLSourceClaims. SQLRoot is just a wrapper node.

3. Document Target Namespace should match the namespace declared in your stored procedure and schema. In this case, it should be set to `http://Company.BizTalk.SQLSource`.

4. The SQL Command is the full execute statement that you would use in SQL Enterprise Manager to run your stored procedure. If you have a parameter, you can specify it here. For example, to call the stored procedure that was created, this property would be set to "exec RetrieveClaimData". Or, if you had a parameter specifying the Trading Partner name to query, you could hard code it here as "exec RetrieveClaimData 'TPName'". In the case of a hardcoded parameter, you would want to create one SQL Receive Port per trading partner.

5. The URI can be set to anything, as long as it is unique. Something descriptive can be helpful, such as SQL://SOURCEDB/EDI/TradingPartnerName.

6. Set the Receive Pipeline on the Receive Location to XMLReceive.

7. After you have the SQL Receive Port fully configured, you can enable it and immediately see data arriving on the BizTalk Message Box (assuming there are results available). You may not have a subscriber set up yet, so the data will suspend, but you'll know your data is being retrieved successfully.

File Send Port

The File Send Port is set up to push out a single 837P file whenever data comes in on the SQL adapter. This means that if the SQL Adapter is set up to trigger every 15 minutes, a file could be written every 15 minutes (assuming there is data returned). This File Send Port should be set up as follows:

1. Create a Send Port called Company.BizTalk.Send.TradingPartnerName. X837P.Unbatched.

2. Set the Send Pipeline to EdiSend.

3. Set the Type to File and write this file to a directory on your computer.

4. On the Outbound Maps tab, select the map you created in Company.BizTalk. Maps.X837.Outbound. The source and target document schemas should automatically be selected when you choose the map.

5. On the Filters tab, set the following property: BTS.ReceivePortName == Company.BizTalk.Receive.SourceSQLXML.

6. Starting this Send Port now allows you to test that every time the SQL Receive Port returns data it gets successfully mapped and transformed into an individual ST/SE 837P document. The actual batching of the data happens in the following components.

File Receive Port

The second receive port in this pattern is the File Receive Port, which picks up the individual 837P documents that are created each time the SQL Receive Port executes and returns data. When this File Receive Port picks up the data, the batching settings on the BizTalk Party Agreement cause the document to queue up and not be delivered until the batch executes. Setting up this Receive Port can be done using the following steps:

1. Create a new Receive Port and Receive Location combination, both named Company.BizTalk.Receive.TradingPartner.ToBeBatched.

2. Set the Type to File and point it to the directory where the File Send Port is writing out the individual 837P files.

3. Set the Receive Pipeline to EdiReceive.

> **Note** There is no requirement that you design your batching outbound flow using this exact pattern of Send and Receive Ports. It is possible to batch without ever physically writing out the individual 837P documents to a file directory. However, by splitting the steps into smaller pieces, you'll find that development, testing, and troubleshooting are greatly simplified because you have access to the document at all stages of the cycle.

SFTP Send Port

The final Port created is the SFTP Send Port that delivers the batched data out to the trading partner. This Port needs to be configured in conjunction with the Batch configuration on the BizTalk Party—it references properties set in the configuration, and the configuration references this Send Port. The SFTP Send Port listens directly to the BizTalk Message Box for the batched 837P EDI file that was created when the Agreement's Batch triggered it (see the next section for details on this configuration). The Send Port uses several filters, and can be configured using the following steps:

1. Create a new Send Port named Company.BizTalk.Receive.TradingPartner. Batched.

2. Set the Type to SFTP. Details for configuring the SFTP adapter are given in Chapter 5.

3. Set the Send Pipeline to EdiSend, or to a custom pipeline that replaces the GS08 version with the appropriate value.

> **Note** The GS08 and batching 837P 5010 documents have proved interesting. You may find that your data always fails batching due to a generic error. If you are certain that your configuration is correct, check the version in the GS08 on your outbound individual EDI document written by the File Send Port. If it is 005010X222A1, you may find that you need to set it to 005010X222 in the original outbound File Send and replace it with the correct value of 005010X222A1 in a custom pipeline on the final outbound SFTP Send Port. This is likely a bug in BizTalk Server batching, and may be corrected with a future patch.

4. On the Filters tab, set the following filters:

   - EDI.ToBeBatched == false
   - EDI.BatchName == TradingPartner_Professional [should match the batch name configured in the Agreement]
   - EDI.DestinationPartyName == TradingPartner [should match the value of DestinationPartyName on the Identifiers tab of the BizTalk Agreement]

The final two bullets listed here are critical to the success of your batching. It can get complicated when dealing with multiple document types across multiple parties that have various batch configurations. In the case of the solution at hand, the DestinationPartyName property on the Identifiers tab in the Agreement that contains the Batch settings is only set for batching purposes. You will not have set this property unless you are configuring batching. The values for both can be anything that you want them to be, they just have to match exactly with one another.

Batch Settings in the Party Agreement

In the previous chapter, you looked at configuring the base settings for the BizTalk Party and Agreement on inbound data. You don't need to configure any new parties or Agreements for the outbound solution, but you need to configure these same settings on the tab that represents the outbound data, from the Company party to the Trading Partner party.

After you have the envelope settings and various core settings configured (which should match almost exactly what you have for the inbound settings), you can look at configuring the actual batch—which is unique to this outbound solution.

To configure the batch, open the Agreement you created in Chapter 2 and take these steps:

1. On the Identifiers tab of the Agreement, set the DestinationPartyName to TradingPartner. This needs to be a unique value across all your trading partners.

2. On the Batch Configuration tab of the Agreement, click the New Batch button.

3. Set the Batch name property to TradingPartner_Professional.

4. Set the Batch filter property with the following filters:

5. BTS.ReceivePortName == Company.BizTalk.Receive.TradingPartner. ToBeBatched [this should match the name of the File Receive Port you created earlier in this chapter]

6. EDI.ST01 != 997

7. Use the Scheduler to configure the appropriate outbound schedule. In the case of this solution, the batch should go out every 24 hours or once a day at a specific time. You can set this to whatever is required for your solution. When the specified time comes, if anything has queued up since the last time the batch executed, it will be immediately released.

> **Note** During development and testing, you will find that clicking the Override button on the Batch will be of great help. It forces a batch to be produced as soon as it is clicked.

8. Click Start to allow the batch to begin processing. You may have to click OK or Apply and reopen the Agreement to get the batch to fully start. It can take several minutes the first time to get started.

9. Check the running instances in your BizTalk Group Hub reports to ensure that your batch is started—you will see an orchestration running for every batch that you have started.

10. Click the Send Ports tab of the Agreement and select the SFTP Send Port you created earlier in this chapter—Company.BizTalk.Receive.TradingPartner. Batched.

11. Click OK to save all your settings.

> **Note** Getting the batch and Send Port to align with one another may take several stops and starts of the batch and of the BizTalk Host Instance. The batch functionality is pretty impressive, and it works great once it is running, but it can take some patience to get it right when you are first setting it up.

Enabling and Running the Solution

For this solution to work, both of the Receive Locations must be enabled, both of the Send Ports must be started, and the BizTalk Batch on the Agreement must be running. You want to restart the BizTalk Host Instance to ensure that all the most recent configurations and components are loaded into memory.

Conclusion

This chapter covered some critical aspects of developing BizTalk EDI solutions within the health care space—most notably batching data and structuring your outbound data in SQL Server to prepare it for mapping. You will likely find that the requirements for your specific implementation vary from the specific pattern outlined in this solution, but you should have more than enough information now to architect an efficient and highly maintainable outbound solution.

Mapping Data Chapter 4

Constructing and deconstructing the data in the various EDI formats associated with health care is a task that requires both analysis and development skills. There are people within claims management who specialize in working with data as it is defined in the various formats, and someone acting as an EDI analyst will be critical during initial inbound and outbound BizTalk map implementations.

It is possible to look at an implementation guide and make intelligent decisions about how data should be mapped, but without the EDI analyst testing and reviewing the data, the chances of getting a fully compliant document that your trading partner can consume is unlikely. To improve your chances for a compliant EDI document early in the development process, take the following steps:

- Whenever possible, get access to an actual EDI document that is being used for the specific trading partner you are working with. Implementation guides are good for reference, but as a developer, having access to the actual file is of immense value. It allows for side-by-side comparisons between what you are creating in BizTalk and what you know is a valid format.

- There are many alternative ways to populate data in the 837 Professional, Institutional, and Dental formats, and it is common to have mapping requirements that are unique to a trading partner. Be prepared to have maps that are very different between partners, whether inbound or outbound.

- Different trading partners require different levels of validation on data delivered to them. BizTalk supports level 1 and level 2 of HIPAA compliance validation. If more levels of compliance are required, you will need to create your level 2 compliant document in BizTalk and then deliver the final file (individual or batched) to another application that will perform the additional levels of validation.

- The work of creating an outbound 837 document from scratch requires both a developer and an EDI 837 Analyst. The developer focuses on the BizTalk map implementation, while the EDI Analyst works with the developer to unit test the data. The testing portion of mapping health care EDI data, especially when dealing with the 837 formats, takes as much time as the actual development. Don't underestimate the need for this resource—only rarely will you find someone who can do both development and full analysis and testing of this type of data.

- In some cases, mapping is best done in multiple stages. It is always nice to be able to map a source document to the target EDI document (or vice versa) in a single map, but it does not always allow for the easiest or most maintainable solution. When developing your maps, think about the next person who may have to take over these maps from you at a later time. Will they be able to interpret what you have done and make modifications to it, if needed? When planning your mapping, think about ways to simplify your logic, and determine if creating several maps that take the data through several phases of transformation could ease your development.

The topics in this chapter cover how to approach mapping the 837 Professional format with several development techniques. It won't be possible to demonstrate how to map an 837 document in its entirety, but with some key foundational information available and some patience, you will be able to create maps that are well architected and use the most appropriate mapping technologies.

Note When building outbound maps in which you have control over the source data from which you are mapping, try to pre-format as much data as possible so that once it gets to the BizTalk map, there is as little additional mapping needed as possible. The less complex your map is, the easier your solution will be to develop, test, and maintain.

BizTalk Mapping Technologies

There are several technologies that you need to be comfortable with the tools available in BizTalk to handle the complex mapping associated with working on 837 document implementations. The BizTalk Visual Studio map is the canvas for development, but there are numerous options for mapping the data. These mapping technologies are as follows:

- *Functoids.* There are many functoids available to you, and it is possible to implement almost all the 837 mapping requirements without the use of external scripts. However, trying to implement an 837 map without the use of external scripts is a mistake, and will lead to an enormously complex map.

- *Inline .NET code.* The Scripting functoid in the mapper allows for a variety of scripting languages. You can accomplish quite a bit within these scripts, but you have limited access to libraries. Only those libraries available to XLANG can be used within a Scripting functoid.

- *External .NET Assemblies.* When you need the power of the full .NET engine and associated libraries, you'll want to develop an actual assembly with methods that can be called from the map. Some tasks - such as interactions with a database—are often best done in external assemblies.

- *Inline XSLT.* This is a very important skill to develop, and should not be overlooked or avoided. Tasks that could take many functoids or complex external .NET scripts can be done quickly using XSLT. Some mapping issues in more complex documents can't even be solved without the use of XSLT. While there will be some ramp up in learning this scripting language, it will be worth your investment.

- *External XSLT.* In most cases, you will use the functoids and mapping options available in the map to complete your solution. In other cases, you may want to simply create a shell to an external XSLT file to handle the mapping.

- *SQL Stored Procedures.* When dealing with business rules, data level transformations, or lookups, you may want to embed the logic within stored procedures. Calling a stored procedure through an external .NET assembly from a map is an easy architecture to build and can be of great benefit.

Looking at actual examples of mapping technologies is what this section is devoted to. With these specific examples in front of you, you should be able to jump into the development of your 837 health care maps with a solid direction as to how to implement. You'll look at two sets of examples—data being mapped to an outbound 837P and data being mapped from an inbound 837P.

Mapping to an Outbound 837P

Mapping to an 837P from an internal data structure is required whenever you are sending outbound data. The solution outlined in Chapter 3 discusses creating the internal data structure from a SQL Server stored procedure, but of course source data could in reality come from a variety of sources - flat files, internal 837 documents, and various databases, just to name a few. In the end, you will always be mapping from a source structure to the target 837 P schema, and the mapping requirements will be similar regardless of the actual source of data.

Formatting Dates Using an External .NET Assembly

There are a large number of date fields in an 837 document that have to be populated. Take the scenario where the source data was generated by SQL Server and all dates are in the format similar to 2012-10-21T04:00:20.043. The target date fields (such as BHT04) need to have this format converted to 20121021. This formatting must be applied to many fields, and the code used to convert from the SQL format to the EDI format needs to be used each time.

There are many options for implementation, including using standard functoids, but the most appropriate solution that uses the least amount of components is an external .NET assembly. If standard functoids were used, you would have to use several string functoids in a pattern, and this pattern would have to be applied over and over in the map. With the external .NET assembly, the code is written once, and a Scripting functoid is dropped wherever the conversion needs to take place. If the conversion logic needs to be changed for whatever reason (such as the source data format changes), then it only has to be changed in one place (the referenced DLL) and not everywhere the conversion is taking place (which would be the case with the functoid pattern).

To build this using an external .NET assembly, take the following steps.

MAPPING WITH AN EXTERNAL .NET ASSEMBLY

This exercise walks through calling an external assembly to format dates in EDI compliant formats.

1. Create a .NET class library. Give it a namespace of Maps.Helper, and a class name of Helper.

2. Create a method called FormatDate that has one input parameter in string format. Write the code to convert from the source format to the target EDI format. An example of this code is shown in Listing 4-1.

3. Compile the assembly and reference it in your Visual Studio map project.

4. In the map, drop a Scripting functoid on the map surface. Drag the input from the source document's date field, and drop it on the target document's date field.

5. Open the Scripting functoid and click the Script Functoid Configuration tab. Set the script type to External Assembly, then select your Script assembly, class, and method from the drop-downs. If your assembly is not shown, try closing Visual Studio and reopening. In some cases, you may have to install the DLL to the Global Assembly Cache (GAC— see next step) to see it.

6. Test the map. This requires that the assembly be deployed to the GAC. Chapter 2 discusses how to deploy assemblies via the BizTalk Administration Console, which places them in the GAC.

An example of this functoid being used on the BHT04 field is shown in Figure 4-1.

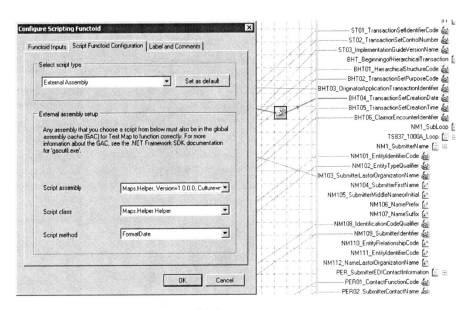

Figure 4-1. Calling an external assembly from a map

Listing 4-1. Formatting a Date

```
public string FormatDate(string dateString)
{
 if (string.IsNullOrEmpty(dateString) == false)
 {
 try
 {
 DateTime date = XmlConvert.ToDateTime(dateString,
 XmlDateTimeSerializationMode.Local);
 return date.ToString("yyyyMMdd");
 }
 catch
 {
 return string.Empty;
 }
 }
 else
 {
 return string.Empty;
 }
}
```

Creating HI Records Using Inline XSLT

These 837 documents have a long list of HI records that can be populated and code nodes that can be populated. HI records include diagnosis codes, condition information, and other repeating data types. This example looks at one option for mapping the diagnosis codes (referred to as the HI_HealthCareDiagnosisCode in the 837P BizTalk schema) using Inline XSLT. The Inline XSLT looks at the source data and creates the target data XML based on what is present. Assuming that the source data structure for Diagnosis code is that shown in Figure 4-2, the XSLT in Listing 4-2 can be used to populate the HI node structure in the target 837 Schema shown in the map in Figure 4-3. Note that there is no input to the Scripting functoid that contains the Inline XSLT.

Figure 4-2. Diagnosis code structure in the source data

Listing 4-2. Inline XSLT for Diagnosis Code Creation

```
<xsl:element name="ns0:HI_HealthCareDiagnosisCode">
 <xsl:for-each select="//*[local-
name()='DiagnosisCode']">
 <xsl:if test="./@SequenceNumber = '1'">
 <xsl:element name="ns0:C022_HealthCareCodeInformation">
 <xsl:element name="C02201_DiagnosisTypeCode">BK</
xsl:element>
 <xsl:element name="C02202_DiagnosisCode"><xsl:value-of
 select="translate(.,'.','')"/></xsl:element>
 </xsl:element>
 </xsl:if>

 <xsl:if test="./@SequenceNumber = '2'">
 <xsl:element name="ns0:C022_
HealthCareCodeInformation_2">
 <xsl:element name="C02201_DiagnosisTypeCode">BF</
xsl:element>
 <xsl:element name="C02202_DiagnosisCode"><xsl:value-of
 select="translate(.,'.','')"/></xsl:element>
 </xsl:element>
 </xsl:if>

 <xsl:if test="./@SequenceNumber = '3'">
 <xsl:element name="ns0:C022_
HealthCareCodeInformation_3">
 <xsl:element name="C02201_DiagnosisTypeCode">BF</
xsl:element>
 <xsl:element name="C02202_DiagnosisCode"><xsl:value-of
 select="translate(.,'.','')"/></xsl:element>
 </xsl:element>
 </xsl:if>
 </xsl:for-each>
</xsl:element>
```

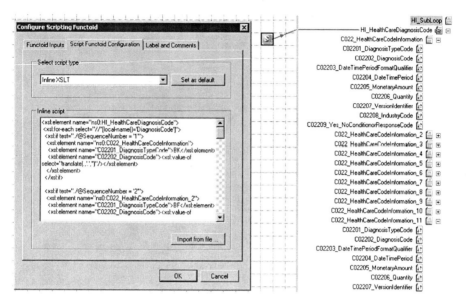

Figure 4-3. Mapping to the HI_HealthCareDiagnosisCode using inline XSLT

The XSLT is looping through all the source diagnosis codes available in the source data and creating target codes in the 837 EDI document in the exact XML structure that matches the schema. Only one XSLT script is required for mapping all these nodes. Depending on the SequenceNumber of the source code, the appropriate target code is created in the EDI document. The translate() method in the XSLT is used to remove periods from the source data before placing it in the target data.

Inline XSLT is amazingly useful with BizTalk mapping, and 837 data in particular. It gives the level of control over parsing and manipulating data that is essential. Looking throughout the source data, regardless of where data lies in the overall hierarchy and node structure, allows for building the logic that may be required without having to build ridiculously complex functoid pattern solutions.

Service Line Mapping Using Inline XSLT Call Template

In the previous example, you looked at Inline XSLT, which does not require any inputs to the Scripting functoid. Inline XSLT can parse through the source data without reference to anything. However, in some cases you may need to pass in one or more parameters. A great of example of this is in the case of Service Line mapping, which can be very involved. You may decide that the entire Service Line detail, from the TS837_2400_Loop down, is best created using XSLT. In the case at hand, the source data contains many claims, and each claim contains one or more service lines. To successfully map the target loop, the Transaction ID of the source claim data needs to be passed into the Inline XSLT Call Template so that only those service lines associated with the specific claim being mapped at this specific time in the map are copied over.

The code in List 4-3 shows a snippet of how a parameter can be passed, and how the Service Line in the target schema can be created. The TID parameter is passed in from the source. The xsl:if then checks to see whether that TID matches the current data's TID (each would have a unique ID). If so, the service line gets mapped, otherwise it is ignored, as it belongs to some other claim.

Listing 4-3. Passing a Parameter into Inline XSLT Call Template Code

```
<xsl:template name="ServiceLine">
 <xsl:param name="TID" />
 <xsl:for-each select="//*[local-name()='ServiceLine']">
 <xsl:if test="../../../*/*[local-name()='TransactionID']
= $TID">

 <xsl:element name="ns0:TS837_2400_Loop">
 <xsl:element name="ns0:LX_ServiceLineNumber">
 <LX01_AssignedNumber>
 <xsl:number /> <!-- will create numeric for this line,
ordered -->
 </LX01_AssignedNumber>
 </xsl:element>
        . . . . . . .

        </xsl:element>
        </xsl:if>
        </xsl:for-each>
        </xsl:template>
```

HL Hierarchy Mapping with Functoids

Setting the HL01 and HL02 values can be a little daunting when creating an out-bound 837 document from a source document that doesn't contain hierarchy relations. The best way to set your hierarchy values accurately is through the use of a Loop functoid (which you will likely have to loop through all the source data to get it into the target data) and two Scripting functoid shapes. Assuming that the Loop functoid is mapped to your target TS837Q1_2000A_Loop, all HL hierarchy nodes in the target document can be set using the same two functoids. The first functoid sets the value of the HL01, and the second functoid sets the value of the HL02. Every HL01 in the target schema should have its source as the HL01 functoid, and every HL02 should have its source as the HL02 functoid. This means both of them will have many outputs. Neither has an input. Instead, the HL01 functoid declares a global variable that is available to other functoids within the map, and the HL02 functoid has access to this global variable.

The code for the HL01 functoid is shown in Listing 4-4, and the code for the HL02 functoid is shown in Listing 4-5. This code is added as Inline C# into the respective functoids. Figure 4-4 shows the functoid configuration in the map.

Listing 4-4. The HL01 Functoid

```
// global variable
int intHL01;

// this gets executed on every HL01 mapped to
public int getHL01()
{
  intHL01++;
  return intHL01;
}
```

Listing 4-5. The HL02 Functoid

```
// references global variable set and declared in HL01
script
public int getHL02()
{
  return intHL01 - 1;
}
```

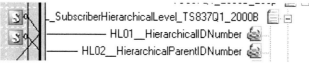

Figure 4-4. Mapping HL Segments

Mapping from an Inbound 837P

Mapping from an inbound 837P to a flat file or other format required by systems within your company requires some analysis. You want to ensure that your maps are as simple, efficient, and easily maintainable as possible. This may require that you use several maps to split out the mapping into logical steps, rather than trying to force everything into a single map. It may also mean you rely heavily on XSLT in the map, and don't depend too heavily on standard functoids. Given the complexity of the 837 formats, it is extremely easy to end up with a map that is completely unusable and unsupportable. What you do not want to end up with is a map that looks like that shown in Figure 4-5.

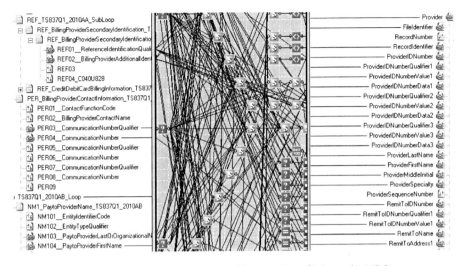

Figure 4-5. An unsupportable and unacceptable mapping of inbound 837P Data

To avoid ending up in a scenario like that shown in Figure 4-5, take the following steps:

- *Plan your architecture—wait to start development.* It is easy and tempting to just start mapping. Eighty percent of the mapping you'll do with an inbound 837 is straightforward, and you'll find that you make quick progress with much of the implementation. Given the size of it, 80% of the mapping will be hours' worth of work. Then, as you begin on the final 20%, you'll start to run into hurdles that are very difficult to overcome, especially if you haven't built the rest of your map to support this 20%. You'll find that loops you've built and nodes you've mapped have to be rewritten to support your requirements. So, in short, plan your mapping before you start development.

- *Start with the most complex nodes first.* Assess what is the most complicated aspect of mapping, and deal with that first. It will ensure that you are developing with the right approach. If you find that you have to rethink your approach, you haven't wasted a lot of time on other mappings.

- *Use XSLT.* There are so many complexities in mapping the 837 that are reduced and simplified by using XSLT that it is a mistake not to plan on using it extensively in your maps.

The technologies used for mapping are outlined in the earlier section on outbound mapping, and are the same for inbound. Here are several examples of mapping inbound data that you can use.

Using More than One Map to Handle a Single Map Case

There are times when it is critical that you use multiple maps to map a single inbound 837 document to an internal format. The case of the ECSIF format was mentioned in Chapter 2. This format is nearly as complex in nature as the 837P, and contains virtually all the same information. Like the 837P, the ECSIF format is also a flat file format. To use two maps, you'll need three schemas. You need to work with two of these schemas whether building a single step map or multiple maps. These are the schema that match the inbound 837P and the outbound ECSIF flat file format. The third schema is an intermediary schema that is a half-way structure between the 837 and the final ECSIF, formed in such a way as to aid in the transformation.

An example of using three schemas and two maps for mapping the Inbound 837 to a flat ECSIF file structure is shown in the following figures. The first figure (Figure 4-6) shows a partial shot of the map from the 837P structure to the intermediary ECSIF schema. Figure 4-7 shows the mapping between the intermediary structure and the final ECSIF flat file structure.

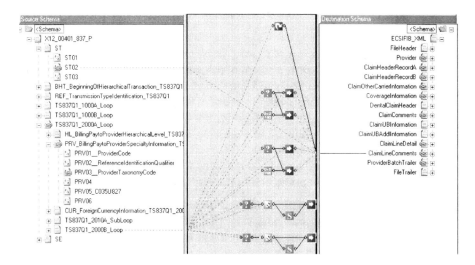

Figure 4-6. The first map—837P to ECSIF intermediary

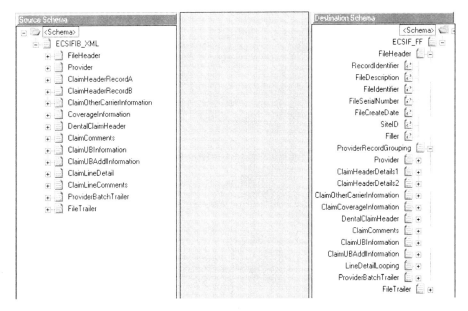

Figure 4-7. The second map—ECSIF intermediary to ECSIF flat file

When using two or more maps for a single mapping requirement, you will most likely want to incorporate an orchestration. The orchestration allows you to stack your maps one after the other. If you were just using one map, an orchestration would not be required, as the mapping could be done directly on the ports. Figure 4-8 shows the pattern for developing an orchestration with the two maps.

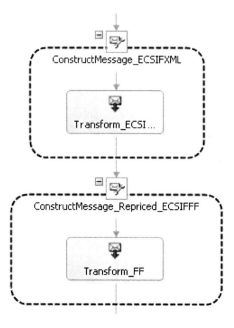

Figure 4-8. An orchestration with the two maps for ECSIF transformation

Using an External XSLT File for Mapping

There are two examples of using Inline XSLT earlier in this chapter, both of which could be used in conjunction with traditional mapping. There is one other type of mapping that can be used when things are simply unmanageable within a map. This option is to shell out to an external XSLT solution and skip the BizTalk mapper completely. Refer to Figure 4-7 and notice that there are no mappings showing in it. This is an example of a map that uses external XSLT. To use external XSLT, take these steps:

- Open up a text editor and create your XSLT. An example of an XSLT file that can be used as a template in your development is shown in Listing 4-6.

Note Using an external XSLT file for mapping means that you do not have to use the BizTalk mapper interface in Visual Studio to test your maps. There are a number of free tools available on the Internet that allow you to specify a source XML document to map from and an XSLT file to use to generate test output data.

- Create a new BizTalk map. Click anywhere on the map surface and select properties. Set the Custom XSL Path to the location of the XSLT you just created. For simplicity, add the XSLT file to the Visual Studio project at the same level as this map. The file can then be referenced as .\CustomXSLT.xslt.

Listing 4-6. Template for an External XSLT File

```
<?xml version="1.0" encoding="UTF-16"?>
<xsl:stylesheet xmlns:xsl="http://www.w3.org/1999/XSL/
Transform"
 xmlns:msxsl="urn:schemas-microsoft-com:xslt"
 xmlns:var="http://schemas.microsoft.com/BizTalk/2003/var"
 exclude-result-prefixes="msxsl var s0" version="1.0"
 xmlns:ns0="http://Company.BizTalk.Schemas.ECSIFOB_FF"
 xmlns:s0="http://Company.BizTalk.Schemas.
ClaimsIB_ECSIF_XML">

 <xsl:output omit-xml-declaration="yes" method="xml"
version="1.0" />
 <xsl:template match="/">
 <xsl:apply-templates select="/s0:ECSIFIB_XML" />
 </xsl:template>

 <xsl:template match="/s0:ECSIFIB_XML">
 <ns0:ECSIF_FF>

 <!-- Your XSLT Code Goes Here -->

 </ns0:ECSIF_FF>
 </xsl:template>
</xsl:stylesheet>
```

Conclusion

This chapter details how to create and map your health care claims. A number of specific examples have been given that should aid you in your development, and the idea that XSLT is one of the most important skills you can bring to the table with 837 mapping has been introduced. Mapping is the most development intensive aspect to the BizTalk solution that you will have, unless you are required to build custom pipeline components. The next chapter details how to configure the various BizTalk components required for health care EDI solutions.

Chapter 5

Ports, AS2 and Acknowledgements

The actual receipt and delivery of files is central to any solution. The most common approaches to receiving and sending data within the EDI Health Care space include SFTP, encrypted data over standard FTP, and secure communications over AS2. SFTP is a simple custom adapter setup and configuration. Dealing with encrypting and decrypting data over FTP requires custom code. Configuring AS2 for direct party-to-party communication requires certificates and complex configurations within BizTalk. This chapter details the set up and configuration for each of these methods, as well as how to successfully deliver various forms of EDI acknowledgements.

SFTP

SFTP is an excellent option for exchanging health care EDI documents, as it is HIPAA compliant and easy to implement. SFTP allows documents to be sent and received in plain text, as the protocol itself encrypts the information (with standard FTP, encrypting the file itself is required to be HIPAA compliant). There are several options for sending and receiving data via SFTP in BizTalk Server, but the recommended approach is to use the third-party bLogical BizTalk SFTP adapter (Blogical. Shared.Adapters.SFTP) available from CodePlex. This adapter is available free of charge and is very reliable. It can be downloaded, compiled, and made available within BizTalk Server within a few minutes.

> **Note** The SFTP adapter automatically downloads the original host certificate from the party you are interacting with. However, if this certificate expires (which is common), the SFTP adapter won't automatically be able to download the new certificate. If you get an exception in the Windows Event Log that says "HostKey does not match previously retrieved HostKey" you will need to browse to the sftphostfiles.config file and delete the HostKey setting. The directory where this file is located is in the Local Settings of the host user that the SFTP adapter runs under. For example, if your BizTalk Host instance runs under DOMAIN\Host_User_Account, then you will browse to Host_User_Account\Local Settings. The config file is buried under a unique directory several levels below, so you need to run a search for it once you have located this directory.

Configuring the SFTP Adapter

After the adapter has been installed, setting it up to receive and send data can be done by creating a new receive location or send port and setting the Type property to SFTP (or what it was named during the installation). You can then click Configure. Configure the SFTP adapter with the key fields shown in this section. In some cases, you will need to configure additional fields than what is shown here, but in most cases these are all that is required.

Some of the properties listed (such as the Schedule) are unique to the receiving of data. As you configure your SFTP send port or receive location, you'll be able to easily identify which properties apply.

> **Note** Before you configure your SFTP adapter, be sure and test connectivity to the target SFTP site through a standard SFTP-compatible FTP utility (one excellent option is FileZilla, which has support for an array of FTP and SFTP connection types). There are a number of things that may require attention before you can connect successfully, and it is much easier to troubleshoot using a client utility than it is through the BizTalk SFTP adapter.

Schedule Property

This setting has some robust functionality for determining the schedule for querying the source SFTP site. Clicking the ellipsis on this property pops up an interface that allows for scheduling on Daily, Weekly, Monthly, or Timely intervals. You will most likely use the timely interval, every *x* number of minutes, for example. In Figure 5-1, you see the property set to poll the source SFTP site every five minutes. In most cases, you pull your EDI data on regular intervals throughout the day, but you need to coordinate with your trading partner to determine whether there are any scheduling windows that should be avoided.

Figure 5-1. Setting the schedule property for Timely polling interval

After Get Property

This property defaults to Delete, which ensures that the file being retrieved is removed from the source SFTP site as soon as it has been successfully received by BizTalk. If there is an error in transmission, the file will remain on the server. In most cases, you will want to leave this set to Delete, but some trading partners provide archiving of data after a certain period of time, so you may want to leave the file on the server to take advantage of this. If this is not set to Delete, you will need to be sure your polling interval set in the Schedule property does not cause this same file to be retrieved multiple times before it is auto archived by the trading partner.

SSH Error Threshold Property

The SSH Error Threshold property can be used to control how many errors can be encountered before the adapter shuts down. It is fairly common to have connectivity issues with SFTP sites, and it would make sense to increase this error threshold to a sizeable amount to account for this. If left at a low number, the adapter may shut down if the source site cannot be reached over a certain period of time.

> ▨ **Note** If the SFTP adapter encounters errors, the exceptions will be logged to the Windows Event Viewer. Be sure and monitor the state of your SFTP ports, as they will automatically shut down if the error thresholds are exceeded.

SSH Host Property

This property should be set with the actual SFTP server host address. This could be an IP or a named server. It should only contain the root server name, not any subfolders. It should also not contain sftp://. An example of this property set to an IP would be 192.168.0.1.

SSH Port Property

The default port for SFTP servers is 22. If you are interacting with an SFTP server that has a different value, you will need to set the appropriate port value here.

SSH Password Property

Set this to the password used for connecting to the SFTP server.

SSH Remote Path Property

If you are receiving data from a subdirectory of the SFTP site, you'll need to set the full path in this directory. Make sure and add a forward slash (/) before any path you enter in this property. The path is based off of the root server - so if your full path is 192.168.0.1/ChildOne/ChildTwo, you should enter /ChildOne/ChildTwo in this property, and enter 182.168.0.1 in the SSH Host property.

SSH Remote File Name Property

The filename can be set using any combination of plain text and BizTalk macros that you may need. Some of the most common macros are shown in Table 5-1. Macros can be combined—if, for example, you want to show the source filename and combine it with the current datetime, you could put a value of %SourceFileName%_%datetime% in the SSH Remote File Name property.

Table 5-1. Common BizTalk Macros

Macro	Description
%datetime%	Creates a string in the format of YYY-MM-DDThhmmss based on the current UTC time of the server. If you want to take into account the local time zone, you can use %datetime.tz%.
%Message_ID%	Setting your target filename with this macro included in it ensures that you will always have a uniquely named file. The Message_ID is the GUID (Globally Unique Identifier) of the message in the BizTalk Message box.
%SourceFileName%	Sets to the value available in the FILE.ReceivedFileName of the adapter picking up the original file. In some cases, you won't have access to the source filename in your send adapter—such as when the data is originating in an orchestration. This macro retains any file extensions that may have been present (such as .pgp or .txt).

There are more macros than are shown in this table, but there are some fairly severe limitations around what you can name files. If you find that the available BizTalk macros are not flexible enough to meet your requirements, you will have to develop a custom pipeline and pipeline component to create your filename. This pipeline can be added directly to the Send Pipeline on the SFTP Send Port.

SSH User Property

Set this to the username used for connecting to the SFTP server.

Trace Property

If you are running into exceptions when the SFTP adapter runs, you may want to set this property to True to log detailed information about what is happening.

Encrypted Data with Standard FTP

Using the Standard FTP adapter to send and receive data with BizTalk is a breeze but dealing with encrypting and decrypting data is not. This section outlines the standard properties used to configure an FTP adapter for sending or receiving data. Additionally, it discusses some of the challenges around custom pipeline and pipeline component development, and shows how to set up a custom pipeline on a Send Port and a Receive Location.

> ■ **Note** You can send encrypted data via the SFTP adapter or any other adapter, but FTP is the most typical protocol requiring encrypted data when dealing with health care data.

FTP Adapter Settings

If you are sending data over FTP, you can create a Send Port in BizTalk and set the Type to FTP. If you are receiving data over FTP, you can create a BizTalk Receive Location and set the Type to FTP. In either case, you will need to set the following key properties:

- *User Name:* The user with which you connect to the FTP site.
- *Password:* The password used for connections.
- *Server:* The FTP server. This should contain the IP or named server being connected to, and should not have the ftp:// prefix on it.
- *Port:* The specific port required for FTP connections.
- *Folder:* The remote folder that you are posting data to. It should not have a leading forward slash (/) on it.
- *Representation:* Binary or ASCII. In general, this should be set to binary, but some FTP servers don't handle binary data, so you may have to experiment with settings here.

With the FTP adapter settings configured properly, you need only to focus on the requirements of the send pipeline.

Pipelines and Pipeline Components

One of the most complex tasks in BizTalk is creating custom pipelines, as it is pure C# development. If you are using PGP for encryption and decryption, some pointers on how to develop this custom pipeline component are outlined in in this section. If you need to use an alternative encryption format, then you'll need to code something specific to the tools that are used for that format. In either case, you'll need someone who is familiar with C# development to be available to work on this.

There are two items that must be set up for both the send pipeline that encrypts data and the receive pipeline that decrypts data. These items are the custom pipeline and the custom pipeline component. The custom pipeline component should be developed first. Let's assume that you are going to be dealing with PGP encrypted data. There are several tools that you could use—one of the easiest to interact with is GNU Privacy Guard (www.gnupg.org). This utility allows for the generation and management of PGP keys, and provides a command line interface that can be communicated with via C# .NET code.

Calling the command line tool requires that you build out a .NET class to wrap the call so that the pipeline can pass parameters to the command line and execute it (using System.Diagnostics.ProcessStartInfo is one option to do this). Assuming you have built a wrapper class for the GNU Privacy Guard command line tool (generally located in the GNU/GnuPG/pub directory), then a sample of calling this command line tool from within a custom pipeline component to encode data is shown in Listing 5-1, while a sample of decoding data is shown in Listing 5-2.

Listing 5-1. Calling a Class to Encode Data with Parameters

```
GnuPGWrapper GPG = new GnuPGWrapper(_gnupgbindir);
GnuPGComm
GPGCommand.Command = Commands.Encrypt;
GPGCommand.Recipient = _recipient; // this is the
recipient on the PGP key
GPGCommand.Passphrase = _passphrase ; // this is the
passphrase on the PGP key
GPGCommand.Armor = true;
GPGCommand.InputFile = inFile;
GPGCommand.OutputFile = outFile;
```

Listing 5-2. Calling a Class to Decode Data with Parameters

```
GnuPGWrapper GPG = new GnuPGWrapper(_gnupgbindir);
GnuPGCommand GPGCommand = GPG.Command;
GPGCommand.Command = Commands.Decrypt;
GPGCommand.InputFile = inFile;
GPGCommand.OutputFile = outFile;
GPGCommand.Passphrase = _passphrase; // this is the
passphrase of the PGP key
```

Creating the custom pipeline component takes some effort, and depends on the encryption and decryption requirements of your solution. You want to make a number of the fields configurable, so that you can use the send and receive pipelines on multiple trading partners. Figure 5-2 shows what these configurable properties could look like when they are set within the custom pipeline in Visual Studio.

⊟ Pipeline Component Properties	
EncryptData	True
GnuPGBinDir	C:\Program Files (x86)\GNU\GnuPG\bin
Passphrase	p@ssword1
Recipient	partnername@tradingpartner.com

Figure 5-2. Configurable parameters on the send pipeline component

The actual custom pipeline where you would be adding the custom pipeline components has to also be created. This is done within Visual Studio as a new BizTalk Pipeline project. An example of a send pipeline and what stage the custom pipeline component to encrypt should be added is shown in Figure 5-3. An example of a receive pipeline and the custom pipeline to decrypt is shown in Figure 5-4.

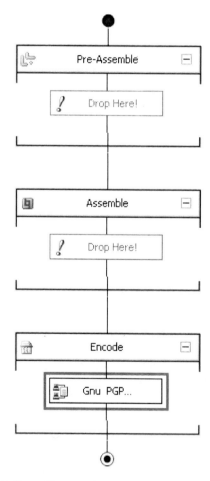

Figure 5-3. The send pipeline with encrypt component

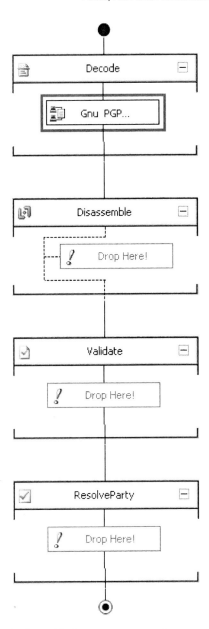

Figure 5-4. The receive pipeline with decrypt component

After you have created your pipelines and deployed them, they will be available to the Send Port and Receive Location where you have configured your FTP adapter. An example of a Receive Location with the decryption pipeline configured on it is shown in Figure 5-5.

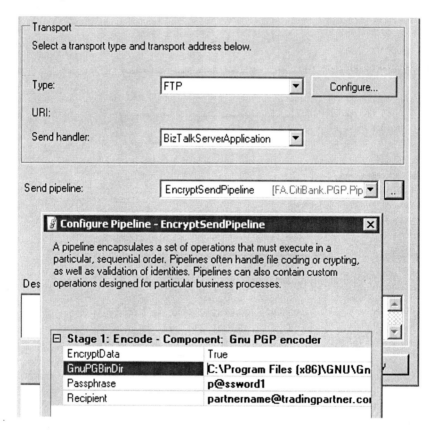

Figure 5-5. Configuring the pipeline on an FTP send port

AS2 Communications

Configuring BizTalk for AS2 communications can be a time-consuming and difficult task. The most complex aspect of it is dealing with certificates. Both you and your trading partner are required to exchange certificates and configure communications with one another with the same settings. Should your data be encrypted? Should your MDN be signed? Do you have the correct certificate for the development environment versus the production environment? Is your trading partner sending data in the expected format? The purpose of this section is to provide you with enough detail around configuring and testing AS2 so that you can avoid most of the pitfalls associated with setting this up.

Certificates

The first thing you want to do is get your certificates set up. Begin by exchanging public keys with your trading partner. You should have a public and private key for your organization and a public key from the trading partner. After you have these, you can take the following steps to set up the certificates on the BizTalk server.

CERTIFICATE CONFIGURATION FOR AS2

This exercise demonstrates where to place and how to reference the certificates required in AS2 communications with BizTalk.

1. Log into the BizTalk server using a BizTalk service account.

2. Open the Certificate manager. From the Start menu, click Run and type **mmc**. Once this is open, click File and select Add/Remove Snap-in. Select Certificates and click Add. Select the My user account option and click Finish. Select Certificates again and click Add—this time, select the Computer account option and click Next. Select the Local Computer option and click Finish. You should now have two Certificate types, as shown in Figure 5-6. After this is complete, click OK.

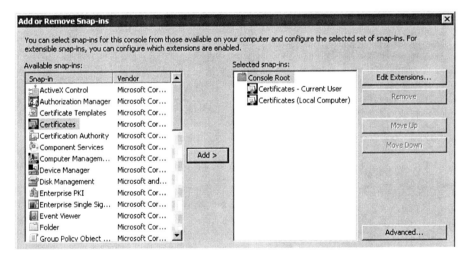

Figure 5-6. Configuring the certificate snap-in

3. With the Certificate console open, expand Certificates Current User, and right-click Personal. Select Import and import the private key (.pfx) for your home organization.

4. Next, expand Certificates - Local Computer, and right-click Other People. Select Import and import the public key (.cer) for your trading partner's organization.

5. You should now see your certificates in several locations—the Personal and Other People folders of both the Local Computer and Current User. With these certificates installed, you now can reference them from the appropriate locations in BizTalk.

6. In the BizTalk Administration Console, right-click the BizTalk Group and select properties. Click the Certificate option and select Browse. Your home organization's certificate should appear, select it and click OK. Figure 5-7 shows the certificate set at this level. This is your primary certificate used to sign outbound data.

> **Note** You can override this default certificate for specific parties, if needed, in the Certificate page of the AS2 properties for your trading partner. In most cases, you'll use a single certificate for everyone, but there may be times when you'll need to use a unique certificate for signing.

Figure 5-7. Batching with multiple claims per ST/SE

7. Right-click your trading partner's BizTalk party in the BizTalk Admin Console's Parties folder and select Properties. Click the Certificate option and click Browse. Select the trading partner's certificate.

There are only two other locations that you may need to configure certificates for your AS2 communications with a single trading partner - on the "Signature Certificate" page of the AS2 agreement (which allows for overriding the default home organization certificate on outbound documents and MDNs) and on any Send Ports that you may be using. However, it is unlikely that you will need to do anything with either of these if you are engaging in standard AS2 communications.

IIS and the BizTalk HTTP Receive Location

AS2 is communication over HTTP, so setting up a site within IIS on the BizTalk Server is a requirement. There are a number of ways this can be set up, but the most common is to create a virtual directory for a specific trading partner that maps inbound requests to the BTSHTTPReceive.dll (which then pushes the inbound data to BizTalk for processing). This is a fairly involved yet easy configuration, and the following exercise outlines how to set up the various components.

> ▦ **Note** In some cases, your organization may not allow companies outside your network to post data directly via HTTP to BizTalk. In this case, you'll have to set up a proxy server to allow traffic to flow through your DMZ and hit the HTTP location in BizTalk. This is a separate area of expertise from BizTalk, and should be handled by a network administrator.

CONFIGURING IIS AND THE HTTP RECEIVE LOCATION

This exercise demonstrates how to create and configure the appropriate IIS components to handle inbound AS2 posts. It also shows how to set up the BizTalk Receive Location that receives these posts.

1. Log in to the BizTalk server using a BizTalk service account.

2. Open the IIS 7 manager, click the root server, and select the Handler Mappings option. In the Actions area on the right side of the screen, click Add Script Map. Set the Request path property to BtsHttpReceive.dll and set the Executable to the location of the BtsHttpReceive.dll (this is located in the HttpReceive folder in the root BizTalk Server directory). Set the Name field to BizTalk HTTP Receive and then click the Request Restrictions button. In the Request Restrictions box, on the Access tab, select Script and click OK.

3. Click OK on the Add Script Map window when this has all been completed. Right-click the BizTalk HTTP Receive item that was just created and select Edit Feature Permissions. In the window that opens, select the Read, Script, and Execute boxes and click OK. See Figure 5-8 for a view of the final configuration.

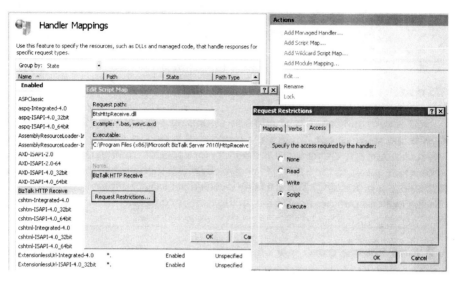

Figure 5-8. Configuring the HTTP receive handler map in IIS

4. Back on the root server in IIS, click the ISAPI and CGI Restrictions icon. In the window that opens, set the BTSHTTPReceive Restriction setting to Allowed, as shown in Figure 5-9.

 ISAPI and CGI Restrictions

Use this feature to specify the ISAPI and CGI extension

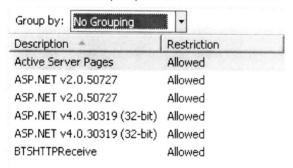

Group by: No Grouping

Description	Restriction
Active Server Pages	Allowed
ASP.NET v2.0.50727	Allowed
ASP.NET v2.0.50727	Allowed
ASP.NET v4.0.30319 (32-bit)	Allowed
ASP.NET v4.0.30319 (32-bit)	Allowed
BTSHTTPReceive	Allowed

Figure 5-9. Configuring the HTTP receive handler map in IIS

5. Create a new Application Pool in IIS, and set the name to BizTalkAppPool (or similar). Set the .NET Framework version property to 4.0 (whichever specific version is available to you) and the Managed Pipeline mode to Integrated.

6. Create a new virtual directory (as an Application) under the Default Web Site. The name of this site should be specific to the trading partner that you will be receiving data from over HTTP—so in this case, name it TradingPartner. Set the Application Pool to the app pool you created in the previous step and select Test Connection to ensure you are able to connect.

> **Note** Depending on your security setting, you may find that you also need to set the Physical Path Credentials to a specific account that has access to that directory. The easiest way to access this is to right-click the web Application you created and select Manage Application and then Advanced Settings.

7. Click the virtual directory you just created and select the Authentication icon. In Authentication window that opens, set Anonymous Authentication to Enabled.

This completes the setup of all IIS related components for AS2. If additional trading partners need to be set up, create one additional virtual directory for each one.

Agreements and Party Settings

To specify how to handle the AS2 data and how to work with the underlying EDI document that is being sent via AS2, you will need to set up a BizTalk Party and two Agreements. One Agreement is for the AS2 messaging, and one Agreement is for dealing with the actual EDI data. The basic steps for setup are as follows for receiving AS2 data from a trading partner (sending data to a trading partner is very similar):

- Create a new BizTalk Party with the name of the trading partner you will be receiving data from.
- If you will be sending a 997 to the trading partner, specify the Send Port that the 997 will be sent out on.

- Create a new Agreement on this Party that will handle AS2 messaging (you can call it something like Agreement_AS2).

- On the General Tab, set the Protocol property to AS2, the First Party to the trading partner, and the Second Party to your home organization. Once you've set the General Tab this way, two additional tabs will appear, one for inbound data from the trading partner, and one for outbound data to the trading partner. If you are just receiving data from the trading partner and returning an MDN, you only need to configure the inbound trading partner tab.

- On the inbound trading partner tab, on the Identifiers tab, set the AS2-From and AS2-To properties to the appropriate values as defined in your trading partner agreement. These must match what is on the AS2 envelope being sent to you. Figure 5-10 shows an example of these settings.

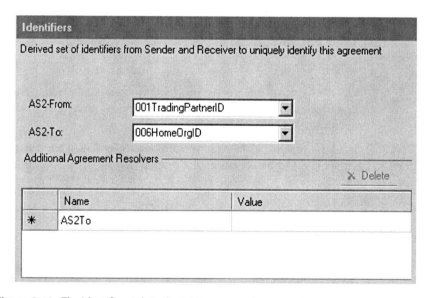

Figure 5-10. The Identifiers tab in the AS2 agreement

- On the Validation tab for the AS2 Agreement, you can set the appropriate values for validation of the data. For example, if you are receiving a signed and encrypted inbound post from a trading partner, then you would set the properties as shown in Figure 5-11.

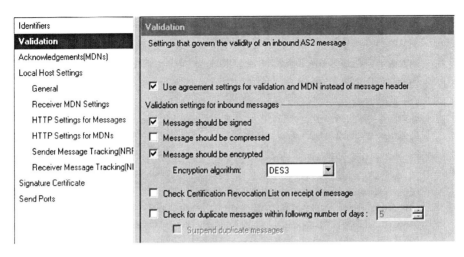

Figure 5-11. The Validation tab in the AS2 agreement

- On the Acknowledgement tab of the AS2 Agreement, you can set the properties that pertain to the MDN response back to the trading partner. If you need to send an unsigned MDN, you can use the properties as shown in Figure 5-12. If you are sending a signed MDN, then the certificate specific in the Signature Certificate settings will be used (or, if none is specified, then the default certificate associated with the BizTalk Group will be used).

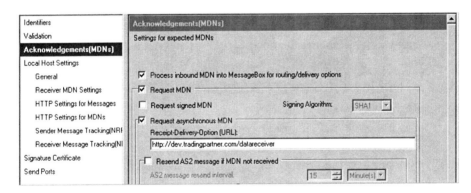

Figure 5-12. The Acknowledgements tab in the AS2 agreement

There are some additional properties that will likely need to be set or adjusted on the other tabs. A few of the most common are noted here:

- On the Receive MDN Settings tab, enable the Sign requested MDN setting if you want to always send an MDN, regardless of what is noted on the inbound AS2 request from the trading partner.

- In the HTTP Settings for Messages, enable everything except for the Ignore SSL Certificate Name mismatch property.

- In the HTTP Settings for MDN, enable everything except for the Unfold HTTP headers property.

- On the Signature Certificate tab, set the certificate that you want to use for signing the outbound MDN. If nothing is selected here, the default certificate for the BizTalk Group will be used.

- Create a new Agreement for the EDI data that will be consumed. Setting this up will depend on the specifics of the EDI document type(s) that are being received over AS2 (you can see details of configuring Agreement settings in Chapters 2 and 3). What is important to know here is that you must have this additional Agreement in place so that BizTalk knows how to process the EDI data once the AS2 Agreement has successfully completed the data transfer.

The Generic MDN Send Port for Asynchronous Messages

The MDN is the acknowledgement for AS2 posts. There are two possible methods for postback of an MDN—synchronous and asynchronous. The synchronous response is posted back via the same open HTTP connection that the original document came in on, and does not require any additional BizTalk components (simply set the Request MDN checkbox in the BizTalk Agreement, and it will automatically post back). For asynchronous MDNs, a send port must be created. You can create a generic send port that will work for all parties by taking a few steps:

- Create a new Dynamic One-way Send Port and name it something such as SendAsyncronousMDNs.

- Set the Filter on the Send Port to EdiIntAS.IsAS2AsynchronousMdn == True.

- Set the Send pipeline to AS2Send.

- In the BizTalk Agreement for AS2, select the Request asynchronous MDN property and set the Receipt-Delivery-Option (URL) property to the URL that the trading partner is expecting data to be delivered on.

When the configuration is set like this, the moment a document is received from a trading partner, BizTalk will automatically create an MDN and drop it on the BizTalk Message Box. The SendAsynchronousMDNs send port subscribes to this document and sends it out to the URL specified in the Receipt-Deliver-Option (URL) property on whatever trading partner's Agreement was just used to receive the data.

Testing Your AS2 Configuration

One of the most challenging (and frustrating) aspects of AS2 configuration is the actual trading partner testing. The best advice is to plan to set up your AS2 configuration in stages. Try to exchange plain text data (unencrypted and unsigned) first before dealing with the various settings requiring certificates. If you can get the plain, unencoded data to flow—and the MDN to return—successfully, then you can move into testing encryption and signing.

There are many things that can go wrong during testing, and the error messages are often very generic and cryptic. The errors could be on your side, or they could be on the trading partner's side. The more you can do to limit what is being tested at any given stage, the quicker you will be able to get to resolution and completion.

Sending 997/999 Acknowledgements

There are several types of acknowledgements that can be sent in response to EDI communications: Functional (997/999), Technical (TA), and MDNs (for AS2). Configuring and sending MDN acknowledgements was covered earlier in the AS2 section in this chapter. Technical Acknowledgements are rarely required, and are identical in setup to the Functional Let's look at sending the Functional acknowledgements for the EDI data itself. The steps to take are as follows:

- Open the BizTalk Party Agreement that relates to the documents and trading partner that you need to set up the Functional Acknowledgement for, click the Acknowledgements tab. Check 997 Expected, as shown in Figure 5-13.

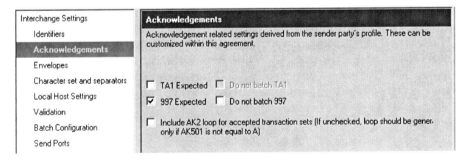

Figure 5-13. The Acknowledgements tab in the EDI agreement

- Set up one Send Port per trading partner. These send ports subscribe directly to the BizTalk Message Box, and filter on the specific trading partner required. The Send Port should have the following settings:
  - The transport type - FTP, SFTP, or other. Set the appropriate connection information for the actual adapter that will be used to connect to the trading partner.
  - The Send Pipeline should be set to EdiSend - or, if you are required to encrypt 997 data (which is uncommon), you will need to add your custom send pipeline to do the encryption.
  - Three filters, as follows:

    EDI.IsSystemGeneratedAck == true

    EDI.ST01 == 997 (or 999 if version 5010)

    EDI.ISA06 == [this should be the specific trading partner's ID that you are configuring for this specific Send Port - this ID can be retrieved from the Party settings of the BizTalk Agreement where you have configured 997s to be sent]

- Depending on your configuration, you may need to associate the 997/999 Send Port with your Agreement on the Send Ports tab.

After you have these settings configured, BizTalk automatically generates a 997/999 when the inbound EDI document is received and drops it on the BizTalk Message Box. Next, the Send Port picks it up and delivers it to the specified destination.

Conclusion

This chapter discussed the most common transport mechanisms for any BizTalk EDI health care implementation you may need to build out. It has also shown how to deal with acknowledgements—997/999s and MDNs. With the information related to AS2, SFTP, and encrypted data over FTP that has been covered, you can develop and interact with trading partners with ease.

Index

CPSIA information can be obtained at www.ICGtesting.com
Printed in the USA
LVOW101342210413

330169LV00014B/498/P